Sweeter than Honey

Sweeter than Honey

Symbolic Numbers and Structure in Psalm 19

Loren F. Bliese

RESOURCE *Publications* • Eugene, Oregon

SWEETER THAN HONEY
Symbolic Numbers and Structure in Psalm 19

Copyright © 2025 Loren F. Bliese. All rights reserved. Except for brief quotations in critical publications or reviews, no part of this book may be reproduced in any manner without prior written permission from the publisher. Write: Permissions, Wipf and Stock Publishers, 199 W. 8th Ave., Suite 3, Eugene, OR 97401.

Resource Publications
An Imprint of Wipf and Stock Publishers
199 W. 8th Ave., Suite 3
Eugene, OR 97401

www.wipfandstock.com

PAPERBACK ISBN: 979-8-3852-5787-4
HARDCOVER ISBN: 979-8-3852-5788-1
EBOOK ISBN: 979-8-3852-5789-8

VERSION NUMBER 10/02/25

Unless identified differently, quotations herein come from the New Revised Standard Version (NRSV) copyright © 1989 National Council of the Churches of Christ. Used by permission. All rights reserved worldwide.

Scripture quotations marked (RSV) are from the Revised Standard Version copyright © 1946, 1952, and 1971 National Council of the Churches of Christ in the United States of America. Used by permission. All rights reserved worldwide.

I dedicate this book to Edith Marie (Albers) Bliese, my beloved wife for 68 years, especially for her faithful love through 44 years in Ethiopia and now in retirement in Oregon. She has been God's special gift to me, and a blessing for many during her service in Ethiopia, especially doing famine relief and later starting private schools. She is amazing, and a really good cook too.

Contents

Chart of the Hebrew Alphabet with Both Numerical Values | ix
New Revised Standard Version English Text of Psalm 19 | xi
Masoretic Text of Hebrew for Psalm 19 | xiii
Preface | xv
Abbreviations | xvii
Introduction | xix

Methodology of Identifying Symbolic Numbers | 1

Overall Structure of Psalm 19 | 6

    Description of a Highly Symbolic Cluster in Ps 19:6B–8A | 9

    Table with Ratios of Symbolism in Cola and Lines 6B–8A | 11

Line-by-Line Analysis of Psalm 19 | 11

    Two Metrically Distinct Poems; the First is Homogeneous and the Second Chiastic | 11

Poem One, 19:1–6: Six Hexameters with the Second Stanza Enclosed by Trimeters | 12

    Two Tables Analyzing Types of Symbolic Lemmas for the 1st Poem Ps 19:1–6 | 25

Poem Two, 19:7–14: Chiasm 555554 4 455555 and a Final Trimeter | 27

    Table 1: Types of Symbolic Factors in poems Ps 19:1–6 and 7–14, and Total 1–14 | 39

Four Tables of Clines of Symbolic Lemmas and Symbolic Factors in Ps 19 | 43

    Table 2: Cline of Ratios of *Alphabetical* Number Symbolism by Poetic Lines | 43

    Table 3: Cline of Ratios of *Mathematical* Number Symbolism by Poetic Lines | 45

Tables of Clines Including Cola Totals for Symbolic Lemmas and Factors | 47

    Table 4: Cline of Mathematical Counts of Lemmas and Factors Plus Cola Totals | 47

    Table 5: Cline of Alphabetic Counts of Lemmas and Factors Plus Cola Totals | 50

Position in the Clines and Numeric Embellishment in Structure for the 22 Lines | 52

How Would an Author Create Such Numerical Embellishments? | 75

The Relationship of Psalm 19 to Psalm 119 with reference to "Fear of the Lord" | 76

Bibliography | 83
Author Index | 87
Subject Index | 89
Scripture Index | 91

Chart of the Hebrew Alphabet with Both Numerical Values

Hebrew	Transliteration	Alphabetical Value	Mathematical Value
א	ʔ	1	1
ב	B	2	2
ג	G	3	3
ד	D	4	4
ה	H	5	5
ו	W	6	6
ז	Z	7	7
ח	ḥ	8	8
ט	ṭ	9	9
י	Y	10	10
ך/כ	K	11	20
ל	L	12	30
ם/מ	M	13	40
ן/נ	N	14	50
ס	S	15	60
ע	ʕ	16	70
ף/פ	P	17	80
ץ/צ	ṣ	18	90
ק	Q	19	100
ר	R	20	200
ש/שׂ/שׁ	ś/š	21	300
ת	T	22	400

HOW LETTER VALUES ARE APPLIED TO WORD VALUES

The sum of the values of the letters in words or lemmas (lexical roots) is their value and in the text below are indicated by an equal sign followed by the value, such as *YHWH*=26 for the sums of *Y*=10, *H*=5, *W*=6, and *H*=5. When both values are included, standard-mathematical values are put in brackets [26] after ordinal-alphabetical values.

New Revised Standard Version English Text of Psalm 19

1*The heavens are telling the glory of God,
and the firmament proclaims his handiwork.
2*Day to day pours forth speech,
and night to night declares knowledge.
3 There is no speech, nor are there words;
their voice is not heard;
4*yet their voice goes out through all the earth
and their words to the end of the world.

In the heavens he has set a tent for the sun,
5*which comes out like a bridegroom from his wedding canopy,
and like a strong man runs its course with joy.
6*Its rising is from the end of the heavens
and its circuit to the end of them,
and nothing is hid from its heat.

7*The law of the Lord is perfect,
reviving the soul;
the decrees of the Lord are sure,
making wise the simple;
8*the precepts of the Lord are right,
rejoicing the heart;
the commandment of the Lord is clear,

enlightening the eyes;
9*the fear of the Lord is pure,
enduring forever;
the ordinances of the Lord are true
and righteous altogether.
10*More to be desired are they than gold,
even much fine gold;
sweeter also than honey
and drippings of the honeycomb.

11*Moreover, by them is your servant warned;
in keeping them there is great reward.
12*But who can detect one's own errors?
Clear me from hidden faults.
13*Keep back your servant also from the insolent;
do not let them have dominion over me.
Then I shall be blameless
and innocent of great transgression.

14*Let the words of my mouth and the meditation of my heart
be acceptable to you,
O Lord, my rock and my redeemer.

Masoretic Text of Hebrew in Psalm 19

1 לַמְנַצֵּחַ מִזְמוֹר לְדָוִד׃
2 הַשָּׁמַיִם מְסַפְּרִים כְּבוֹד־אֵל וּמַעֲשֵׂה יָדָיו מַגִּיד הָרָקִיעַ׃
3 יוֹם לְיוֹם יַבִּיעַ אֹמֶר וְלַיְלָה לְּלַיְלָה יְחַוֶּה־דָּעַת׃
4 אֵין־אֹמֶר וְאֵין דְּבָרִים בְּלִי נִשְׁמָע קוֹלָם׃
5 בְּכָל־הָאָרֶץ ׀ יָצָא קַוָּם וּבִקְצֵה תֵבֵל מִלֵּיהֶם לַשֶּׁמֶשׁ שָׂם־אֹהֶל בָּהֶם׃
6 וְהוּא כְּחָתָן יֹצֵא מֵחֻפָּתוֹ יָשִׂישׂ כְּגִבּוֹר לָרוּץ אֹרַח׃
7 מִקְצֵה הַשָּׁמַיִם ׀ מוֹצָאוֹ וּתְקוּפָתוֹ עַל־קְצוֹתָם וְאֵין נִסְתָּר מֵחַמָּתוֹ׃
8 תּוֹרַת יְהוָה תְּמִימָה מְשִׁיבַת נָפֶשׁ עֵדוּת יְהוָה נֶאֱמָנָה מַחְכִּימַת פֶּתִי׃
9 פִּקּוּדֵי יְהוָה יְשָׁרִים מְשַׂמְּחֵי־לֵב מִצְוַת יְהוָה בָּרָה מְאִירַת עֵינָיִם׃
10 יִרְאַת יְהוָה ׀ טְהוֹרָה עוֹמֶדֶת לָעַד מִשְׁפְּטֵי־יְהוָה אֱמֶת צָדְקוּ יַחְדָּו׃
11 הַנֶּחֱמָדִים מִזָּהָב וּמִפַּז רָב וּמְתוּקִים מִדְּבַשׁ וְנֹפֶת צוּפִים׃
12 גַּם־עַבְדְּךָ נִזְהָר בָּהֶם בְּשָׁמְרָם עֵקֶב רָב׃
13 שְׁגִיאוֹת מִי־יָבִין מִנִּסְתָּרוֹת נַקֵּנִי׃
14 גַּם מִזֵּדִים ׀ חֲשֹׂךְ עַבְדֶּךָ אַל־יִמְשְׁלוּ־בִי אָז אֵיתָם וְנִקֵּיתִי מִפֶּשַׁע רָב׃
15 יִהְיוּ לְרָצוֹן ׀ אִמְרֵי־פִי וְהֶגְיוֹן לִבִּי לְפָנֶיךָ יְהוָה צוּרִי וְגֹאֲלִי׃

Preface

IN THIS STUDY I have investigated the role of numerical patterns in Ps 19, showing how symbolic numbers enhance structural and thematic high points by their higher percentages of symbolic numbers. This is a different way to analyze numerical enhancement in Hebrew scripture than is found in other applications that do not systematically relate percentages of symbolic numbers to structural high points.

While working in Africa as a United Bible Societies' Translation Consultant, I wrote papers distinguishing chiastic texts that have a central peak, and serial texts with a final peak. After retirement, I have been adding symbolic number analysis to these structural studies. In two previous studies, I dealt mainly with numerical values of the Hebrew consonants based on the order of the 22 letters of the alphabet (See 2018 *Count God In: Theological Numbers in the Song of Songs,* and 2021 *God's Good Covenant: Poetic Beauty in Hosea Enhanced by Counting*). In this study of Ps 19, all lexemes/lemmas were counted by both the *alphabetically* ordinal and standard *mathematical* values of the Hebrew letters.

Lemmas with numerically symbolic totals of their letters, and lemmas with symbolic factors were identified for both counting systems with computer help. The symbolic numbers used are those recognized by Labuschagne and other scholars as symbolic by relating to the value 26 of *YHWH* and its associated theological numbers, or 22 of the Hebrew alphabet, or to the wholeness number 7.

The next step in the research was to add the symbolic alphabetical and mathematical lemma totals separately for every colon and line. Ratios of symbolic lemmas and factors for each poetic line were then calculated by dividing the number of symbolic lemmas and factors by the total number of lemmas. This gave data for comparison with other lines. The ratios were put into four tables of clines with varied ways of counting, and evaluated for each line to identify high and low ratios.

One of the outcomes of this process was that a group in vv. 6B–8A proved to have higher than average percentages. Each line has ratios of 200% or more, meaning twice as many symbolic factors as lemmas. The location is significant because these lines come at the juncture of the two poems in Ps 19. The first of these lines, 6B, is the final peak of the first poem, and 7A–8A are the first three lines of the second poem with the theme of the Torah. The fact that these structurally significant lines have high ratios is strong evidence that structure is marked by numerical symbolism in Ps 19

Further evidence of numerical marking comes with lemmas with many symbolic factors. Such lemmas are especially interesting when they are repeated in the psalm in places of special meaning. For example, there is an inclusio of "heavens" as the first word in the first poem, coming again in its final v. 6. Another example is "hide" in the final peak 6B, which connects the "sun" from which nothing is "hidden," with God who clears "hidden faults" in v. 12.

The overall structure is also more clearly defined. There are 22 lines pairing into 11 two-line strophes. They form two poems, 19:1–6, and 19:7–14, each with two stanzas. The first poem has 4 strophes that end with a final peak. The second has 7 chiastically balanced strophes, with 3 strophes on each side of the central peak strophe in v. 10.

A very interesting outcome was the discovery that the line with "fear of the Lord" in 9[10]A has a very high percentage. This is discussed in the paper's final section in terms of not being one of the Torah words in Ps 119. Many other structurally significant places with numerical marking are presented in detail in this study.

Abbreviations

BDB	Brown, Driver, Briggs. *A Hebrew and English Lexicon of the Old Testament*
GNT	*Good News Translation*
MT	Masoretic Text (from *Biblia Hebraica Stuttgartensia*)
NRSV	*New Revised Standard Version*
RSV	*Revised Standard Version*
SIL	Summer Institute of Linguistics
UBS	United Bible Societies
v.	verse
vv.	verses
//	is used to separate parallel units

(In tables some words have been shortened to fit the margins:)

fact. or fac.	factors
lemm. or lem.	lemmas
lwst.	lowest
Mathem.	Mathematical
monoc. or mc. or m.	monocolon
Sym.	Symbolic
Theol.	Theological

Introduction

THIS STUDY AIMS TO show how *number patterns* are part of the inventory used to add beauty and emphasis in Psalm 19. This book's title, "Sweeter Than Honey," comes from 19:10, referring to the "ordinances" of the Torah. In a broader application, the Word of God is loved and is "sweeter than honey" to God's people because of its message. This study will develop a special characteristic of scripture that authors added to mark high points and make scripture aesthetically "sweet"—embellishment by symbolic numbers. Numerical embellishment is found in much of scripture, and especially in Wisdom poetry like Ps 19.

As an example, the word *mtwq* 'sweet' has the highest count with six symbolic factors, including two alphabetical for 60 (10x6), and four mathematical for 546 (26, 13, 6, and 7). This makes *mtwq* one of the most powerful symbolic words in Ps 19. The four factors as well as six internal factors are listed in the footnote below.[1] Beyond the large number of factors, there is a unique application of number symbolism with the location of two 546s. The sum of the mathematical values of all the word roots in the line ahead of "sweet" is 546, giving it a numerical connection to "sweet," the first word of 10B. Significantly, the line with the total of 546 is the *peak line 10A of the poem on the Torah*. This use of identical consecutive

---

1. The factors of 546 are 26x21, 13x42, 6x91, and 7x78. All of the first numbers of these four double factors are symbolic—26 is the value of God's name YHWH, 13 and 6 are also related to YHWH, and 7, which is also a factor of the second numbers of the above first three, 21, 42, and 91, is a symbol of "fullness." The number 78 is powerful with YHWH numbers 26x3 and 6x13. The number 546 also has factors of 39x14, with 39 being special both as 13x3 and as the sum of 26+13, and 14 is symbolic as 7x2. This is a rich and "sweet" mixture of *YHWH* numbers and the fullness number seven, without any numbers from the 22-set.

INTRODUCTION

symbolic numbers brings together the two lines that are the climax of the praise of God's word in the Torah: "More to be desired are they than gold, even much fine gold; sweeter also than honey and drippings of the honeycomb." Numerical embellishment adds sweetness to the structure of the poem as well as to the message.

The presence of symbolic numbers is well documented in biblical Hebrew and other ancient languages.[2] Numerical enhancement is in addition to well-known poetic features in biblical Hebrew, such as parallelism, cohesion, meter, and sound patterns, and will be shown to interact with them, adding further prominence. Special attention will be given to how numerical embellishment highlights *structural and thematic high points*. This will be done by comparing numerical symbolism in tables with descending clines of the percentages of symbolism in each poetic line.

We will now look at some general numerically symbolic patterns in Psalm 19. The two adjacent lines in Ps 19:3–4A each have 26 Hebrew letters. Since 26 is the numeric value of *YHWH*, this sparked an interest to see what other symbolic numbers can be identified in the psalm, and how they might add to understanding its structure and message. Other numerical patterns emerged. The first section, 1–6 [Hebrew 1–7], including the introduction, has 78 or 26x3 lemmas/lexical roots. If the three words of the introduction are not counted, the first poem 1–6 [Hebrew 2–7] has 51 words or 17x3 ending on its final peak. 17 is the short count for *YHWH*, as will be explained below. The first word in the second poem is "Torah" in verse 7 [8]. It is the keyword of the second poem. Its position as the 52nd word is significant since 52= 26x2.[3] It seems likely that the knowledge of

---

2. Lenzi ("Placement of Psalms 19 and 119," 458) writes: "Attributing significance to numbers and numerical patterns within a text was commonplace throughout the entire ancient world." Lenzi references studies of number symbolism in Akkadian, Babylonian, Assyrian, and biblical Hebrew. Knohl ("Sacred Architecture," 189-197) shows patterns with 52, 26, and 17 in word and cola counts in four biblical poems outside of the Psalms, and in Ps 92. He notes that all occur in MT but some do not occur in the Samaritan Pentateuch, which raises the question of the age of biblical symbolic numbers.

3. See Zinner ("Introduction." *Numerical and Acrostic Techniques*, 9).

the highly symbolic numbers 51 and 52 influenced the number of words at the juncture of the two poems.

A number that shows embellishment by its repetition is 6, the value of *W* found in *YHWH*. It involves words rather than lemmas. The first section, including the introduction through the end of the first poem at v. 6, has 54 words or 6x9. The second poem in vv. 7–14 [8–15] has 72 words or 6x12. Adding them together for the total of the psalm gives 126 with factors 6x21, and also factors 7x18 with the fullness number 7. The number 126 is also interesting since its digits contain the number 26, although this use of symbolic numbers within larger numbers is not seen to be as productive as the others.

Significantly, there are 22 poetic lines, resembling many biblical poems (19 of the 22 lines are bicola and three are monocola).[4]

The main numeric data for this study was extracted from the lemmas or lexical roots behind the surface words in the Hebrew of Psalm 19. The value of each letter was counted and added up to calculate the total for each lemma. To find which lemmas were numerically symbolic, these totals were checked against a list of symbolic numbers used in numerological studies in biblical Hebrew.[5] The discussion "Verse by Verse Analysis" will provide details of these lemma counts and their factors, and after the tables of clines comes a discussion, "Position in the Clines and Numeric Embellishment in Structure for the 22 Lines."

---

4. The word "colon" (plural "cola") refers to the basic unit of a poetic line. "Monocolon" refers to a line with one colon, and a bicolon has two cola, which is the usual structure of a poetic line. Verses are normally made of one or two lines, but may be several lines. Pss 33 and 103 have 22 verses. Ps 38 has 22 lines after the introduction. Pss 111 and 112 have 22 cola with the first letters acrostic. Freedman (*Psalm 119*) analyzes Pss 111, 112, and 119 along with others based on the 22-letter alphabet.

5. For the theoretical basis of biblical symbolic numbers, see Labuschagne (*Biblical Arithmology*). Zinner ("Psalm 19," 16) in Table 1 presents a list of both "Standard Gematria" and "Ordinal Gematria" in Psalm 19. For lists of symbolic numbers and the reasons for their symbolism, see Bliese (*Song of Songs*, 4-6), Bliese (*Hosea*, 7-8), and pp. 2-4 below.

Methodology of Identifying Symbolic Numbers

HOW ARE SYMBOLIC NUMBERS identified in this paper? Hebrew did not have symbols for numbers, so the alphabetic letters were also used as numbers. Originally, the value of a letter was its sequential order in the alphabet. Later, to signify larger numbers, the eleventh letter *kap* was counted as twenty, and the following letters became the decimals from 30 to 90, and the last four (*q, r, ś/š, t*) became hundreds from 100 to 400. The higher values of mathematical counts became "standard" in Hebrew numerical gematria (applying numbers to letters) and later Kabbalah mystical applications, which were especially developed in the Middle Ages and continue to the present.[1] The use of both counts in Ps 19 is clearly shown in this study.[2]

    1. A very interesting study using the mathematical count for Hebrew symbolic numbers is by Oscar Goldberg ("Zahlengebäude" 1908) showing the use of 26 as the number occurring as a factor of the sums of the value of the letters in the names of the consecutive generations of Isaac 8x26, Jacob 7x26, and Joseph 6x26, and of the total of the values of the names of the first 13 descendants of the 26 descendants of Shem in Gen 10:21-29 as 138x26, and of the last 13 as 106x26. He also notes total counts for the text such as number of words equaling 4x26, and of letters 15x26. For a summary of Goldberg's data see Ziemer ("Zahlensymbolik," Section 13), and Krawczyk ("Number 26," 354-361). This amazing data indicates that the larger mathematical values (not just the smaller alphabetical sequence values) were in use at the time of the formation of the text of Genesis. Goldberg's data should be taken into account in exegetical and historical studies of Genesis, and the dating of the mathematical expansion of the use of letters for numbers. Kabbalah also uses sums of the letters for surface *words*. This can result in larger numbers that are more difficult to calculate, and since they obscure the relationship of the lemma behind them to other words with identical lemmas, they have not been analyzed here.

    2. Zinner ("Psalm 19", 25) gives examples of combinations of standard and ordinal gematria counts in Psalms 19, 48, and 85, and notes, "The use of two different systems of gematria, standard and ordinal, in one psalm is not

Three groups of symbolic numbers are used in this analysis. The *theological* group relates to the divine name *YHWH*=26, its prime number base 13, and the short count 17 for *YHWH*. The group includes 10, 5, and 6, the values of the letters in *YHW(H)*, and the *kbwd* 'glory' derivatives 23 and 32, which are based on the construct *kbd*'s highly symbolic values of 17 (alphabetical) and 26 (mathematical) as in the two counts for *YHWH*, so 23 and 32 are recognized as divine-name numbers.

The main *YHWH* values of 26 and 17 gain power by being the same in both alphabetical and mathematical counts since their four letters have values of 10 or less. The short count 17 comes from substituting *aleph*, which has the value of one, instead of Y with its value of 10, relating to God's name in Exo 3:14 *ʔhyh* 'I am', which begins with *aleph*.[3]

The second group has 22 and 11, based on the 22 letters of the Hebrew alphabet. The third group is numbers with factors of the fullness number 7.

Evidence for the fact that *lemmas* were used for counting by biblical authors is found in symbolic numbers of total lemmas in books, especially for keywords. For two examples with the symbolic number 22 based on the 22 alphabetical letters, Deuteronomy has 22 lemmas of the verb *ʔhb* 'love,' but with various verbal forms. Hosea has the lemma *šwb* 'turn' 22 times, making it symbolic. However, the surface forms have a variety, with fourteen occurring only once and four occurring twice each.[4] These examples illustrate how

---

unprecedented."

3. Zinner (*Numerical and Acrostic Techniques*, 25–26) shows the amazing use of symbolic numbers based on divine names in Exo 3:25-26, and that they are mimicked by both LXX and Vulgate translators, indicating their knowledge of Hebrew symbolic numbers.

4. One of those occurring twice is especially interesting. It is *yšbw* and comes in Hos 3:5 and 14:7[8]. It is written without the medial letter *w* in contrast with the same word in 7:16 as *yšwbw*. All three are qal imperfect 3 masculine imperfect verbs. The value of *yšwbw* is 45, with a symbolic factor of 5. However, by writing it without the middle *w* the value becomes 39 with the powerful symbolic factor of 13, the prime number base of the 26 set. 39 is also the sum of 26 plus 13, which gives 39 a very strong symbolism, much more than the 5 of 45. If we look for a reason why two forms are written with this

METHODOLOGY OF IDENTIFYING SYMBOLIC NUMBERS

book totals are consistently based on counting lemmas for designating symbolic numbers.

Most symbolic numbers have theological values linked to 26, which is the value of the divine name YHWH 'the Lord'. They and their multiples make up 90 of the 113, or 79.65% of alphabetical symbolic lemmas in Psalm 19. Some theological lemma values include supplementary factors of the other symbolic sets of 22 and/or 7; for example šmš=55 'sun' in v. 4 with a theological factor of 5 as well as an alphabetical factor of 11, and dʕt=42 'knowledge' in v. 2 with a theological factor 6 as well as a 7. The Hebrew alphabet has 22 letters, and 22 is frequently found in Hebrew poetry, such as in acrostic poems. Therefore, 22 is counted as symbolic along with its prime number base 11 and their multiples. Of the 113 symbolic lemmas, 17 or 15.04% have a factor of 11, placing them in the 22 group. The number 7 is also frequently used in poetic structures focusing on fullness, so it and its multiples are also counted as symbolic.[5] Of the 113 symbolic lemmas, 14 or 12.39% have a factor of 7. Mathematical counts have a total of 110 symbolic lemmas, of which 93 or 84.55% are theological, 11 or 10% are with the 22-set, and 16 or 14.55% are with factors of 7.

While the large counts of mathematical numbers make it more difficult to calculate, some are easily found if an author is looking for a symbolic lemma for embellishment. If a lemma comprises a

---

special symbolism and one is not, the context and the location of the two are significant. Both 3:5 and 14:7[8] are promises of "return" for Israel, while 7:16 condemns Ephraim with "they do not turn upwards". The symbolic 39 gives special marking to the positive promises. The location in the book of Hosea of both of these positive promises is also significant. Verse 3:5 is the end of the first block of 88 poetic lines, and 14:7[8] is the third verse from the end of the book in a final section describing the blessings of the return. So the positive closures of the first block and of the whole book are both marked by the short form yšbw with the value of 39. I propose that this is a numerical embellishment given to God's role in the return from exile.

5. Labuschagne ("Compositional Techniques," 8) notes that the author of Ps 19 "made the fullest possible use of the number 7 to symbolize the 'fullness' and 'abundance' of God's presence and the blessings of the Torah." Among other examples, Labuschagne points out that "The psalm has 14 (2 x 7) Masoretic verses; there are 7 occurrences of the name YHWH".

combination of only letters from the thirteen letters from y=10 to t=22, it will be symbolic by having factors of both 10 and 5. This makes many lemmas have factors with the value of the letters of YH. For example, the mathematical factors for the lemma in the first word of Ps 19 *šmym*=390 'heavens' are 26x15, 13x30, 10x39, 6x65, and 5x78. The second lemma *spr*=340 'declare' has 17x20, 10x34, and 5x68. Both of these have 10 and 5, plus other symbolic numbers. There are 43 of the 167 lemmas with only these 13 letters in Ps 19. Similarly, an h=5 along with a combination of only any of the 13 letters with final zeros will always have the symbolic factor 5. For example, the lemma in the first word of the second line has *mʿśh* 'work' =415 5x83. In 4A and 6A *qṣh* =195 'end' comes three times with factors of 5x39 and 13x15. There are ten lemmas in Ps 19 with an h=5 plus a combination of the 13 with final zeros, and another five lemmas of article h 'the' =5.

The research methodology was first to analyze the values of all lemmas in Ps 19. This began with adding both the alphabetical and mathematical values of the letters of each lemma. The lemma values were then checked to see if they were multiples of any of the symbolic numbers by dividing each of the eleven symbolic numbers 26, 13, 17, 23, 32, 10, 6, 5, 22, 11, and 7 into each lemma value to identify its factors. For example, 13 is the prime number base of the 26 set, so *spr* 'tell' =52 in v. 1 is also symbolic by having factors of 13x4 and 26x2. When a lemma has the exact value of 26 or 22, whose symbolism is the reason for their sets, but which are not prime numbers, both 26 and 22, as well as their prime numbers 13 and 11 have been counted as symbolic factors in the counts below. For example, both *YHWH*=26, and its prime number 13 are counted as symbolic factors, and both 22 and 11 are counted for *br* 'pure' =22 in v. 8. This gives recognition to the fact that lemmas with the exact value of 26 and 22 have greater symbolism than lemmas with the value of other multiples of their prime numbers 13 and 11.

In this study, only *division* by symbolic numbers was used to determine if a lemma value had symbolism. However, 39 has been noted to have another level of symbolism by the *addition* of

26+13=39 in addition to 13x3=39.[6] This has been noted in parentheses when it occurs.

The "Line-by-Line Analysis of Psalm 19" below was prepared with transliterated Hebrew lemmas followed by the alphabetical and mathematical totals of their letters. All symbolic lemma totals or factors were marked in bold. Colon totals of both alphabetical and mathematical factors were added up, and the sums were checked by the eleven symbolic numbers for symbolism. Ratios of symbolic factors divided by the number of lemmas for each colon were also calculated. Mini-tables with the results were added after each line.

This was followed by creating Table 1 with three lists of the number of symbolic factors for each of the eleven symbolic numbers in the two poems (1) 1–6 and (2) 7–14, and together for (3) all of 1–14. Tables 2–5 have clines of all 22 poetic lines ranking the lines by the ratios from the line-by-line analysis. The cline in Table 2 has the percentages of symbolic lemmas and factors by alphabetical counts, and Table 3 has them for mathematical counts. Tables 4 and 5 add the *colon* total numbers to the lemma and factor counts found in Tables 2 and 3.

After the tables, in "Position in the Clines and Numeric Embellishment in Structure for the 22 Lines," the individual lines are each discussed in terms of their placement in the clines, their major symbolic numbers, parallel repetition of symbolic numbers, and how the numbers relate to the literary structure of the psalm. Identifying patterns of high or low symbolism in regard to structure is a primary goal of this study. Whether or not embellishment of texts by numerical symbolism was planned or by chance, it would likely be part of a number-conscious reader's appreciation, so it is pointed out in this study whenever observed.

---

6. Labuschagne ("Numerical," 128–30) credits Claus Schedl for pointing out that 39 is symbolic as the sum of 26+13, deriving from Deut 6:4 "YHWH (is) one" where YHWH=26 and ʾḥd=13 totaling 39. Bliese (*Hosea*, 20–21) notes that 39, with 76 occurrences in Hosea, is third in the theological set after 26 and 13, which both have 110 occurrences. In his Table 3 with counts of lemmas with the same value, he notes that 38 has only 44 occurrences, and 40 has 46, showing the much larger 39 with 76 occurrences between them.

Overall Structure of Psalm 19

Psalm 19 is often analyzed with two separate metrical units, which is followed here.[7] The first in 1–6 is metrically homogeneous with hexameters. A homogeneous meter typically points to a final peak. Here, the peak is the short trimeter 6B.[8] It is numerically prominent, a high ratio of 200% (5/11) for mathematical counts of factors divided by the number of lemmas in the line. A terrace series of doublets "day–day, night–night" comes in v. 2, and three staircase repetitions ABABAB, with A "goes-forth" and B "end" come in 4–6, all making a buildup to a final peak.[9] The theme of creation, proclaiming the "glory of God" (v. 1) to the "end" (4) of the "earth" is tied to the example of the circuit of the sun going forth (4–5) to the "ends" (6) of the "heavens."[10] The final peak (6B)

---

7. Goldingay (*Psalms*, 285) notes that the first six verses have mainly 3-3 lines, but there is "a marked change of rhythm" in that the rest of the psalm is mainly 3-2 lines. Zinner ("Psalm 19," 2) in a study on the unity of Psalm 19 points to the poetic use of 3-2 Qinah's broader use in Psalm 19 as evidence of Late Biblical Hebrew in both sections. Zinner (*Psalm 119*, 81) also notes Late Biblical Hebrew vocabulary, including *rqyʿ* 'firmament' in Ps 19:1 [2], and on p. 90 "the sense of 'endure' for *ʿwmdt* in Ps 19:9 [10]. On p. 10 Zinner states: "Ps 19 has one author, and he was postexilic." Other views on the structure of Ps 19 include Mathis (*Working Preacher*, "Commentary"), who is among those who suggest the two parts may have originally been two psalms. Klein ("Half Way Between," 138) sees the prayer in the last four verses as a third part and notes, "This tripartite division has long determined the exegesis of Psalm 19." A tripartite structure would not invalidate this study since v. 10[11] would become a final peak rather than a chiastic peak, and the rest of the structural high points would be the same (see p. xvi near the end of the Preface).

8. Craigie (*Psalms 1–50*, 183) emphasizes the importance of v. 6B [Hebrew 7B], "The key clause, as Lewis has pointed out, is in v 7: 'there is none hidden from its (the sun's) heat.' The clause marks the transition between the two parts of the psalm and at the same time links them intimately together.... And as the sun can be both welcome, in giving warmth, and terrifying in its unrelenting heat, so too the *Torah* can be both life-imparting, but also scorching, testing, and purifying."

9. See Bliese ("Symmetry and Prominence," 72–74). Note especially on p. 72, "in homogeneous poems the repeated words are often found in groups leading to the end."

10. Ziemer ("Zahlensymbolik," Section 13) suggests that the placement of Psalm 19 could be related to the 19 years it takes for the convergence of

OVERALL STRUCTURE OF PSALM 19

has 13 letters, which is also used in Hebrew poetry for emphasis since it is half of 26, the value of *YHWH*. An earlier short trimeter comes in 4B, introducing the first poem's second stanza. This fits together with the final trimeter as a discontinuous bicolon enclosing the stanza. These two lines may be seen as having parallelism despite their distance: 4B "in them he has set a tent for the sun," // 6B "And there is nothing hidden from its heat." Strophic structure is consistently doublets throughout the psalm. They are marked below in "Line-by-Line Analysis of Psalm 19" with a + between them. The short monocolon lines are all paired with normal bicola lines, making doublets similar to the strophes with two bicola. Semantic groups (stanzas) are marked with ++; there is one in each poem in this analysis after vv. 4 and 10.

The second poem, in 7–14, can be analyzed as a metrical chiasm with five pentameters on each end and three tetrameters in the center.[11] The central peak in 10A comes at the end of a series of six repetitions of the word "Lord" that are preceded by the genitive of a noun related to the Torah or "teaching." The first four are "Torah," "decrees," "precepts," and "commandments," which are all in Ps 119. Then comes "the fear of the Lord," which is not in Ps 119, and finally "ordinances of the Lord" which is in Ps 119. The departure in the sequence to "fear" rather than the semantic field of legal terms in the others sets it apart semantically.[12]

---

the solar and lunar annual circuits, which was known in ancient times. The semantic group of the movement of sun and moon including both "day" (the time of the sun) and "night" (the time of the moon) in v. 2, "line" of the heavens in v. 4, "end" in v. 4, "run its course" in v. 5, and "circuit to their ends" in v. 6 support this possibility.

11. Goldengay (Psalms, 298) states that in 7-11 the predominantly "3-2 rhythm . . . corresponds to that of Ps 119," but both have many variations.

12. Goldengay (Psalms, 290) notes that all four of the other words in 7–9 have cohesion as "instructions," but that "'Reverence for Yahweh' does not so fit". Goldengay adds, "the occurrence of the term 'Yhwh's reverence' draws attention to the wisdom flavor of vv. 7-11 (cf Job 28:28; Prov. 1:7)." Klein ("Half Way Between", 12) writes, "The fear of Yhwh is a key term in Old Testament wisdom literature. Especially in Proverbs the concept appears as a gateway towards wisdom (Prov 1:7; 2:5; 9:10; 15:33). The insight that the relation with God is a prerequisite for sapiential knowledge is also reflected in the equation

The peak in 10A reads, "They are desired more than gold (*zhb*) even much fine gold (*pz*)." "Fine gold" has the highest symbolic value of 26, giving prominence to the peak. The two peak clauses have parallelism, with the synonyms for gold, and the repetition of the comparison word *than*, which is the preposition *min-* assimilated to nouns. There are 17 letters in this peak (10A), which is the short count for YHWH, often used to mark prominence in Hebrew poetry.[13] The previous six lines in vv. 7–9 have the same parallel form—the first colon beginning with Torah or one of its categories, followed by a characteristic of each, and the second colon describing an activity of each. Yoder and Zinner list the sequence of masculine and feminine nouns in Ps 19:7-9 [8-10] as gender-based parallelism as an "elegant pattern" that "deepens the impression of the composer's deft poetic abilities."[14]

The metrical chiasm 555554 4 455555 is supported by three items with chiastic structure in vv. 7–14. The first is the inclusio of YHWH coming in v. 7 and then in the last line. The second correlates the "fear of the Lord" in 9A with "by them is your servant warned" in 11A. Both of these lines are the second from the

---

of fear of God and wisdom in Job 28:28".

13. Bliese (*Hosea*, 155) points to a 17 in Hos 8:1B-3 that embellishes what he analyses as the central theme of the book. The keywords are "covenant" in 1B, "God" in v. 2, and "good" in v. 3 and were used for the main title of his *God's Good Covenant*. They are all numerically symbolic. The lemma *ṭwb* 'good' has the value of 17 for both alphabetical and mathematical counts. *Bryt* 'covenant' has the mathematical value of 612 or 17x36 balancing the 17 of *ṭwb* on the other side of "God." The factor 36 with its double digit 6x6 recalls the W=6 of YHWH. *ʔlhym* 'God' comes between them in 8:2 having the most highly symbolic total of 26 times in Hosea. This makes a significant triad of divine name numbers with *ʔlhym* 'God' having a 26 as YHWH, and the line on each side of it with the short count for YHWH 17. (Since the 17s come from the mathematical count of both "covenant" and "good," only the alphabetical 17 of "good" was noted in Bliese's discussion, and the beautiful numerical 17-26-17 pattern was missed. This shows the importance of using both alphabetical and mathematical counts in research.)

14. Yoder and Zinner (*Psalm 119*, 32). They describe "gender-matched parallelism" in Psalms 119 and 19 in the first part of their draft book (pp. 1–42). On p. 32, they list the nearly perfect inversion in Ps 19:7-9[6–10] that includes the Tetragrammaton as "[f-m-f-f-m-m-m-m]-m/[f-m-f-f-m-m-m-m]/f-m".

central peak 10A. The next lines moving out are also parallel with v.8B, "the commandment of the Lord is clear (*yšr*), enlightening the eyes", and v. 12, "who can detect their errors? Clear (*nqh*) me from hidden faults." Such word or thematic chiasmus typically accompanies metrical chiasmus.

The final short trimeter line is a secondary peak marked by being only a single colon, and having the divine name *YHWH* with two praise epithets, "my rock and my redeemer." *YHWH* occurs, significantly, the final *seventh* time here after its six occurrences in the first six lines of the second poem. Besides *YHWH*, and "hidden" noted above, coming in both poems of Psalm 19, "word" (*ʔmr*) ties the two poems together, coming in vv. 2, 3, and 14.[15] Also, note the structural similarity that both poems in Psalm 19 end with trimeter lines. The reference to YHWH as "my rock" comes in Ps 18:2 as well as at the end of Ps 19, making a near inclusio for these two adjacent psalms. The repetition adds prominence to this final verse.[16] Also, the total *YHWH* in Psalm 18 is nineteen, which, when added to the seven in Psalm 19, fills the main symbolic number twenty-six of *YHWH*.[17]

Description of a Highly Symbolic Cluster in Ps 19:6B–8A

A major goal of this study is to determine if there is a correlation between high percentages of symbolic numbers and important structural lines. Seven of the 22 poetic lines in Ps 19 have a ratio of 200% or more symbolic factors by mathematical counts. Four come together in 6B–8A. The first two are at the juncture of 6B, the final peak line of the first poem, "And there is nothing hidden from its heat," and 7A, the first line of the second poem, "The law of the Lord is perfect reviving the soul." Both have a high ratio of 220% for symbolic numbers. The high ratios continue with the

15. See Zinner ("Psalm 19," 463).

16. Goldengay, *Psalms*, 283, adds that "servant" is also part of the inclusio. It comes in the introduction of Ps 18 and in the next to the last verse in Ps 19. He adds other vocabulary in common in both psalms.

17. See Zinner ("Psalm 19," 28).

next two lines in the second poem, with v. 7B "The decrees of the Lord are sure, making wise the simple" with 240%, and 8A "The precepts of the Lord are right, rejoicing the heart" with 220%. 8Aa has its first colon with the highest 300% ratio, but the next colon, 8Ab, has only 100%, ending the cluster of lines with over 200%. In contrast, the next three lines are 9A with 166.67%, 9B with only 120%, and 10A with 137%.

Both 6B as the final peak of the first poem, and 7A–B through 8A as the first three lines of the second poem on the Torah ("teaching") are structurally highly important. They therefore serve as examples that support identifying *numerical embellishment in poetic structure*. The spiritual message and further numerical prominence of these lines are also important to note. "Nothing is hid" from the heat of the sun in 6B has a divine application in 12b relating to God cleansing "hidden faults." Verse 12 is marked by a 200% line ratio and one of the two highest colon ratios of mathematical 300% in 12b. The message of 7–8A is reverence and praise for the "law (*twrh*) of the Lord," which is recognized as a very important Wisdom message related to Ps 119.

As a guideline, having cola, lines, or texts with twice as many or more symbolic factors than lemmas, as shown by ratios 200% or greater, is a helpful numerical marker in identifying highlighted places in structure and meaning.[18] Figures for cola and lines in the cluster from 6B to 8A are presented in the table below. Note especially the consistent 200+ percentages for all except 8Ab in the last column of mathematical factors, and the 100% for all mathematical symbolic lemmas for vv. 7–8A. In contrast, alphabetical counts with 100% for lemmas come only in 7Ba, 7Bb, and 8Ab. Alphabetical *factors* have 100% or higher in 6B, 7Ab, 7Ba, 7Bb, 8Aa, and 8Ab. 8Aa has only 66.67% bringing 8Aa+b down to 80%. The low count of 7A is because each colon has only one symbolic lemma. Both of these lemmas have prominence because of standing alone

18. The seven lines in Ps 19 with a ratio of 200% or more will be listed later in the mathematical counts of Table 3 with 7B at 240%, followed by 4B, 6B, 7A, and 8A at 220%, and 10B, and v. 12 at 200%. All but 4B and 6B are in the second poem. Table 4 lists three of these again: 6B with 216.67%, 7A with 214%, and 4B with 200%.

as symbolic and by having values of 26 for *YHWH* and 52 or 26x2 for *npš* 'soul'. This is a unique way of giving special prominence to 7A as the first line of the second poem instead of a high ratio.

Table with Ratios of Symbolism in Cola and Lines in 19:6B–8

	Alphabetical		Mathematical	
	Sym. lemmas	Sym. factors	Sym. lemmas	Sym. factors
6B(monoc.)	3/5=60%	5/5=100%	3/5=60%	11/5=220%
7Aa	1/3=33.33%	2/3=66.67%	3/3=100%	6/3=200%
7Ab	1/2=50%	2/2=100%	2/2=100%	5/2=250%
7Aa+b	2/5=40%	4/5=80%	5/5=100%	11/5=220%
7Ba	3/3=100%	4/3=133.33%	3/3=100%	8/3=266.67%
7Bb	2/2=100%	3/2=150%	2/2=100%	4/2=200%
7Ba+b	5/5=100%	7/5=140%	5/5=100%	12/5=240%
7A+B	7/10=70%	11/10=110%	10/10=100%	23/10=230%
8Aa	2/3=66.67%	3/3=100%	3/3=100%	9/3=300%
8Ab	2/2=100%	3/2=150%	2/2=100%	2/2=100%
8Aa+b	4/5=80%	6/5=120%	5/5=100%	11/5=220%

Line-by-Line Analysis of Psalm 19[19]

Two Metrically Distinct Poems; the First is Homogeneous and the Second Chiastic

> (Note: The following counts are made on lemmas, which means the lexical roots of Masoretic Text forms. The value of a lemma is the sum of the values of its

---

19. The English structural analysis comes from Bliese ("Psalms 1–24," 306–07). The Hebrew verse numbering includes the prose introduction "To the leader. A song of David" as verse one, making numbers in its text one more than in this study. When included they are in square brackets [ ].

letters. *Symbolic* numbers are in bold, including those of lemmas, factors, and colon totals. Transliterated alphabetical lemmas are also bold when they are symbolic. Mathematical counts are in square brackets [ ] after the alphabetical counts. The numbers in parentheses at the end of each English poetic line are the Masoretic Text word count, sometimes followed by a slash and a suggested modification for oral metered performance. The English text is from NRSV. Hebrew words are signified in the English text by hyphens between multiple English words that translate a Hebrew word. An equal sign = signifies a Hebrew hyphen (*maqqep*). Suggested changes are marked by parentheses enclosing a *maqqep* (=) that might be deleted in the count to add a word-stress, or a plus sign enclosed in parentheses (+) to indicate where a hyphen might be added to eliminate a word-stress. Other notes, such as literal translations, letter counts, and chiastic inversions, are in curly brackets { }. A summary mini-table follows the analysis of each poetic line, showing the numerical data of each colon for lemmas and factors by both alphabetic counts on the left and mathematical counts on the right. The ratios calculated by the total number of lemmas for the divisor and the total number of *symbolic lemmas* for the dividend are in the left-hand column of each half. In the right-hand column of each half the ratios are based on the total number of lemmas for the divisor and the total number of *symbolic factors* for the dividend.)

Poem One, 19:1–6: Six Hexameters with the Second Stanza Enclosed by Trimeters

1   The-heavens are-telling the-glory-of=God;
    {AB Subj Obj//}

    and-the-firmament proclaims his-handiwork.
    {work-of(+)his-hands.} {BA //Obj Subj} (7/6)

POEM ONE, 19:1–6

1a   השמים מספרים כבוד־אל

> **h** 'the' =**5** (x1) [**5**], šmym 'heavens' =57 [**390 26**x**15**, **13**x**30**, **10**x**39**, **6**x**65**, **5**x**78**], **spr** 'tell' =**52** (**26**x**2**, **13**x**4**) [**340 17**x**20**, **10**x**34**, **5**x**68**], **kbwd** 'glory' =**23** (x1) [**32** (x1)], **ʔl** 'God' =**13** (x1) [**31**]. Colon totals = alphabetical **150** (**10**x**15**, **6**x**25**, **5**x**30**), and mathematical [**798 7**x**114**, **6**x**133**].

All lemmas are numerically symbolic by the alphabetical count, except *šmym* 'heavens' (note that alphabetical symbolic lemmas are bold). By the mathematical count, that first word "heavens" has a plethora of five theologically symbolic factors, including the most powerful count 26 for *YHWH* and the values of its three unique letters Y=10, 6=W, and H=5. The second word *spr* 'tell' is also highly symbolic with the alphabetical value of 52 or double 26 for the name *YHWH*, and with the mathematical factors of 17, the short count for *YHWH*, and 10 and 5 representing the abbreviation YH for *YHWH*. The fourth word *ʔl* 'God' has the value of 13 or half of 26 and the prime-number base of the 26-set. The presence of *kbwd* in the final phrase of the first colon *kbwd-ʔl* 'glory of God' is also significant since its alphabetical value of 23 and its mathematical value of 32 represent the divine name *YHWH*. This is an extension based on its construct *kbd,* which has 17 alphabetically and 26 mathematically, the short and full counts of the primary *YHWH* values. Although it is a genitive construct, the MT *kbwd* 'glory' follows the tradition in Psalms of being written with a long vowel letter *w*. This makes the first colon total 150 alphabetically, with factors 10, 6, and 5 as with its first word "heavens." The colon sum 798 for mathematical counts has a theological 6, and a 7 suggesting fullness. All these symbolic numbers, except the 7, are from the theological set. (There are none from the alphabetic set of 22.) The theological message of the colon is enhanced by these theological numbers.

    One way to evaluate the level of symbolism in a text is to divide the number of symbolic lemmas by the total number of lemmas. Here, the total of four symbolic numbers, when divided by five for the total lemmas for the colon, gives 80% for the alphabetical count. A second way to show numerical prominence is with the number of factors. The more symbolic factors a lemma or text has, the more symbolism it has.[20] This colon has 5 symbolic factors by the alphabetic count, which, when divided by 5 for the number of lemmas, results in 100%. The mathematical count is double that, with 10/5 or 200%. The 200% coincides with the highly important theological message of this first colon, "The heavens are telling the glory of God." This first colon is the first of several structurally significant places that have ratios of 200% or more. A proposal developed in this study is that *numeric highlighting embellishes structural prominence in a text.*

1b ומעשה ידיו מגיד הרקיע:

w 'and' =6 (x1) [6], **mʕśh** 'work' =55 (5x11) [415 5x83], **yd** 'hand' =14 (7x2) [14 7x2], **ngd** 'proclaim' =21 (7x3) [57], **h**=5 (x1) [5], **rqyʕ** 'firmament' =65 (13x5) [380 10x38, 5x76]. Colon totals =166 [877] (neither is symbolic).

All 6 lemmas in the alphabetical count and all but *ngd* in the mathematical count are symbolic. By the alphabetical count, four are from the theological set relating to *YHWH*, two are from the 7 fullness set, and one is from the 22 set, along with a theological 5. By mathematical counts, four lemmas are theological, and one has a 7.

The total for 1a+b for alphabetic counts of lemma values is 150+166=316 (not symbolic). The mathematical count total is [798+877=**1675** 5x335].

	Alphabetical		Mathematical	
	Sym. lemmas	Sym. factors	Sym. lemmas	Sym. factors
1a	4/5=80%	5/5=100%	4/5=80%	10/5=200%

20. See Bliese (*Hosea*, 14–15) where multiple factors are called "correlaries," and the strong symbolic value of lemmas with many symbolic factors is discussed.

POEM ONE, 19:1-6

	Alphabetical		Mathematical	
	Sym. lemmas	Sym. factors	Sym. lemmas	Sym. factors
1b	6/6=100%	8/6=133.33%	5/6=83.33%	6/6=100%
1a+b	10/11=90.91%	13/11=118.18%	9/11=81.82%	16/11=145.45%

2   Day to-day pours-forth(+)speech,
    and-night to-night declares=knowledge. (7/6)

2a   יום ליום יביע אמר

ywm 'day' =29 [56 7x8], l=12 (6x2) [30 10x3, 6x5], ywm=29 [56 7x8], **nbʕ** 'pours forth' =32 (x1) [122], **ʔmr** 'speech' =34 (17x2) [241]. Colon totals =104 (13x8), and [505 5x101].

2b   ולילה ללילה יחוה־דעת:

w 'and' =6 (x1) [6], **lylh** 'night' =39 (13x3) [75 5x15], l 'to' =12 (6x2) [30 10x3, 6x5], lylh=39 (13x3) [75 5x15], ḥwh 'declares' =19 [19], **dʕt** 'knowledge' =42 (6x7) [474 6x79]. Totals =157 (not symbolic), and mathematical [**679** 7x97].

The lemma totals for v. 2 are alphabetical 104+157=261 (not symbolic), and [mathematical: 505+474=**979** 11x89]. In v. 2a, the value 32 for *nbʕ* 'pours forth' is symbolic as the divine-name number 32 derived from the mathematical count of *kbwd*. The short count 17 for *YHWH* comes in 2a as an alphabetical factor of *ʔmr* 'speech'. The preposition *l* 'to' comes in the parallelism of each colon and has the alphabetical value of 6 and a strong mathematical value of 30 with factors of 10, 6, and 5, the three letters of YHW(H). The repeated word *lylh* 'night' in v. 2b has the value of 39, which has the alphabetical factor of 13 and is also highly symbolic as the sum of 13 and the divine-name number 26. Its mathematical value is 75 with a factor of 5, which is predictable in lemmas made of only those 13 letters whose values end in zero, plus having an *h*=5.

	Alphabetical		Mathematical	
	Sym. lemmas	Sym. factors	Sym. lemmas	Sym. factors
2a	3/5=60%	2/5=40%	3/5=60%	5/5=100%
2b	5/6=83.33%	6/6=100%	5/6=83.33%	7/6=116.67%
2a+b	8/11=72.73%	8/11=72.73%	8/11=72.73%	12/11=109.09%

In the totals for vv. 1 and 2 in the last row of the previous two mini-tables, both alphabetical and mathematical counts are higher in v. 1. This is especially true of the low counts in 2a, the colon nearest to v. 1, with lemmas only 60% symbolic in both alphabetical and numerical counts, and alphabetical factors only 40%. This supports crediting numerical marking by the author to embellish the first verse, and to further highlight it by having low counts in the first colon of the second verse.

+ (second strophe)

3   There-is-no=speech, nor-are-there words;
      their voice is-not heard; (6)
      {v. 3 has 26 letters recalling YHWH=26}

3a   אין־אמר ואין דברים

ʔyn 'no' =**25** (5x5) [**61**], **ʔmr** 'speech' =**34** (17x2) [241], **w**=6 (x1) [6], **ʔyn**=**25** (5x5) [**61**], **dbr** 'word' =**26** (x1, 13x2) [206]. Totals =116 (not symbolic), mathematical [**575 23x5, 5x115**].

3b   בלי נשמע קולם:

bly 'not' =**24** (6x4) [**42 7x6**], **šmʕ** 'hear' =**50** (10x5) [**410 10x41, 5x82**], qwl 'voice' =37 [**136 17x8**]. Totals =111 (not symbolic) [**588 7x84, 6x98**]. Totals for 3a+b 116+111=227, and [575+588=1163] (both not symbolic).

POEM ONE, 19:1–6

All seven of the alphabetical symbolic lemmas in v. 3 have factors in the theological set, including divine-name factors 26 with dbr 'word,' and 17 with qwl 'voice.' In the mathematical set, 3a has only one symbolic lemma, w, with the symbolic factor [6], but in 3b, all three lemmas are symbolic with theological lemmas. The mathematical colon total 575 for 3a has strong theological factors, with a divine-name factor of 23 and two 5s.

	Alphabetic		Mathematical	
	Sym. lemma	Sym. factors	Sym. lemmas	Sym. factors
3a	5/5=100%	8/5=160%	1/5=20%	1/5=20%
3b	2/3=66.67%	3/3=100%	3/3=100%	5/3=166.67%
3a+b	7/8=87.5%	11/8=137.5%	4/8=50%	6/8=75%

Compared with the mini-table for v. 1, the percentages in v. 3 are lower seven times, and higher five times. The very low 20% for both mathematical counts in colon 3a helps to set off the high 200% in v. 1a. Only v. 11a has lower than 20%, with 0% for both mathematical lemmas and factors.

4A   yet-their-voice {Hebrew 'line'}
       goes-out through-all=the-earth,
   and-their-words to-the-*end*-of the world. (6)
       {4A has 26 letters recalling YHWH=26}

4Aa   בכל־הארץ יצא קום

b 'through' =2 [2], **kl** 'all' =**23** (x1) [**50 10x5**], **h** 'the' =**5** (x1) [**5**], **ʔrṣ** 'earth' =**39** (**13x3**) [291], **yṣʔ** 'goes out' =29 [101], **qw** 'line' =**25** (**5x5**) [106]. Totals =123 (not symbolic), and [**207 23x9**].

4Ab ובקצה תבל מליהם

w=6 (x1) [6], **b**=2 [2], **qṣh** 'end' =**42** (6x7) [**195** 13x15, 5x39 (note that 39=26+13)], **tbl** 'world' =**36** (6x6) [**432** 6x72], **mlh** 'words'=**30** (10x3, 5x6) [**75** 5x15]. Totals =116 (not symbolic), and [**710** 10x71, 5x142].

The totals for 4Aa+b are 123+116=239 (not symbolic), and [625+710=**1335** 5x267].

	Alphabetical		Mathematical	
	Sym. lemma	Sym. factors	Sym. lemmas	Sym. factors
4Aa	4/6=66.67%	5/6=83.33%	2/6=33.33%	3/6=50%
4Ab	4/5=80%	8/5=160%	4/5=80%	5/5=100%
4Aa+b	8/11=72.73%	13/11=118.18%	6/11=54.54%	8/11=72.73%

In comparison, v. 1 has higher counts than 4A in 9 counts, whereas 4A is higher only in alphabetical factors in 4Ab. This continues to show the greater symbolism in the first colon of Ps 19. They are equal at 100% for mathematical factors and 118.18% for alphabetical symbolic factor totals.

++ (2nd stanza of 1st poem, each with 2 strophes)

4B *In-the-heavens* {Hebrew 'in-them'}
he-has-set=a-tent for-the-sun, (3)

"In-them" comes at the end of the line in Hebrew and refers to "heavens" as noted in the NRSV footnote. "Heavens" is also the first word in v. 1, making semantic anaphora by the same referent coming in the first line of each stanza. Structurally this trimeter colon forms a discontinuous bicolon with 6B, the trimeter peak at the end of this first poem. Together they make a seventh hexameter line for the poem.

4B   לשמש שם־אהל בהם:

l 'for' =12 (6x2) [30 10x3, 5x6], šmš 'sun' =55 (11x5) [640 32x20, 10x64, 5x128], śm 'set' =34 (17x2 or 17+17) [350 10x35, 5x70, 7x50], ʔhl 'tent' =18 (6x3) [36 6x6], b 'in (them)' =2 [2]. Totals =121 (11x11), and mathematical [1058 23x46 or 23x(23+23)].

All lemmas in 4B except b=2 are symbolic with both alphabetical and mathematical counts. The short count 17 for YHWH comes as a factor for the alphabetical count of śm =34, and also is significant as the sum of 17+17. The 4B colon total 121 has two 11s with the alphabetical counts—a strong number with 11, the prime number base of the alphabetic 22 set. Another 11 comes with šmš=55 (11x5). Since multiples of 22 and 11 are often used in *structural* counts, the three 11s may point to the fact that this is the first line of the second stanza. The mathematical count of 640 [32x20, 10x64, 5x128] for šmš has the divine-name number 32 and the YH numbers 10 and 5. With mathematical counts, the colon total 1058 for 4B has the factors 23x46, with 23 another one of the divine-name numbers. Interestingly, 46 is equivalent to two 23s, similarly to the above 34, which is equivalent to two 17s. This looks like a play on divine-name numbers for emphasis. This is the only line with the three divine-name numbers 17, 23, and 32. The divine name YHWH=26 is represented numerically by three 10s, four 5s, and four 6s among the factors of 4B. This is equivalent to three YHWHs and a YH, adding to the strong divine-name focus of this short line. The divine-name numbers 23 and 32, based on the word *kbwd* 'glory', are highlighted again in this first line of the second stanza. Numerically, the 23 and 32 in both the highly symbolic *kbwd* of "Glory of God" in 1a, and the 32 in šmš in "tent for the *sun*," along with 23 in the colon total in 4B, support seeing an analogy relating the action of the sun to God.[21] This is especially

---

21. Zinner ("Psalm 19", 25) notes that "the standard gematria of 'El, 31, added to the ordinal gematria (*mispar siddar*) of *šemeš*, 55, produces the sum 86 (31+55=86), the standard gematria of 'Elohim." Since both words come in the first poem, in vv. 1 and 4B, this is another numerical connection supporting an analogy between God and the sun.

true since "tent" is used for the Tabernacle, the dwelling place of God, as in Ps 15:1, which has been described as the first line of a chiasm of Pss 15–24, with Ps 19 as the center.[22]

Similarities between 1a and 4B go beyond individual lemma values. Note the almost identical ratios for their cola, copied here from their mini-tables. The only difference is the 200% in 1a and 220% in 4B for symbolic mathematical factors. Since 200% or more is considered to be a marker for high counts of symbolism, the difference is not significant.

	Alphabetic		Mathematical	
	Sym. lemmas	Sym. factors	Sym. lemmas	Sym. factors
1a	4/5=80%	5/5=100%	4/5=80%	10/5=200%
4B	4/5=80%	5/5=100%	4/5=80%	11/5=220%

Common vocabulary between Ps 19:5 about the sun and other biblical passages about God also supports an analogy between them. See Isa 62:5 "as the bridegroom rejoices over the bride, so shall your God rejoice over you" with the same *ḥtn* 'bridegroom' and *śwś* 'rejoice'. There are also many references to God as *gbwr* 'strong man', which is used in v. 5 to describe the sun. For example, Ps 24:8, where it comes twice translated as "mighty": "Who is the King of glory? The Lord, strong and mighty, the Lord, mighty in battle." Isa 42.13, "The Lord goes forth like a soldier," has *gbwr* translated as "soldier" and *yṣʾ* 'go forth' together as in

22. See Brown ("Here Comes the Sun," 259–77), and see Quinn ("Methodology," 21 who has the Hebrew numbers first and English in square brackets): "In Psalm 19, it's the sun that dwells in a *tent* (v. 5[4]); *tent* is a significant lexeme only used of God's dwelling in the psalm group (Ps 15:1), implying an analogy between God and the sun." Sumpter ("Psalms 15–24," 186) shows the chiasm of matching psalms first described by Auffret ("Les Psaumes 15 à 24") and translated by Brown (260).
  A Ps 15 and 24 (Entrance Liturgy)
    B Ps 16 and 23 (Songs of Trust)
      C Ps 17 and 22 (Prayers for Help)
        D Ps 18 and 20–21 (Royal Psalms)
          E Ps 19 (Creation/Torah Psalm)

Ps 19:5. The final peak line of the first poem in 6B is "And there is nothing hidden from its heat." As noted above, "hidden" is also in v. 12b: "Clear me from hidden faults." This can also be applied analogically to the fact that God knows all human faults, and nothing can be hidden from God.[23] The same verb *str* 'hide' comes in Jer 16:17 "For my eyes are on all their ways; they are not hidden from my presence, nor is their iniquity concealed from my sight." Also, Amos 9:3 "Though they hide themselves on the top of Carmel, from there I will search out and take them; and though they hide from my sight at the bottom of the sea, there I will command the sea-serpent, and it shall bite them." These examples show that the vocabulary for the activity of the sun in Ps 19 is also used biblically to describe God's activity.

Alphabetic lemma value totals for the full v. 4A+B are 239+121=360 (10x36, 6x60, 5x72), and mathematical are [1335+1058=2393 not symbolic]. The following mini-table has the totals for both poetic lines in v. 4. Note that 4Aa+b is a full bicolon, while 4B is a monocolon. (In MT 4B is included in v. 4 [Hebrew 5] rather than the new stanza.)

	Alphabetic		Mathematical	
	Sym.lemmas	Sym. factors	Sym. lemmas	Sym. factors
4A	8/11=72.73%	13/11=118.18%	6/11=54.54%	8/11=72.73%
4B	4/5=80%	5/5=100%	4/5= 80%	11/5=220%
4A+B	12/16=75%	18/16=112.5%	10/16=62.5%	18/16=112.5%

The 220% for symbolic mathematical factors in 4B is important since 200% or more is the percentage shared in mainly

---

23. Quinn ("Methodology," 21) continues from the previous footnote, "Internal coherence within Psalm 19 further supports this conclusion. Within Psalm 19, YHWH's activity is united with that of the sun thematically and through the lexeme *hidden* סתר: Just as the sun actively goes from extremity to extremity, and "nothing is *hidden* from its heat" (vv. 5–7[4–6]), YHWH actively discerns all parts of a human heart, including the *hidden* errors (vv. 13–14[12–13]). This analogy depicts YHWH as relentless to deliver his people from sin to present them as blameless and innocent before him (v. 14[13])."

SWEETER THAN HONEY

structurally significant places. Here, it indicates that this first line of the second stanza has been given extra numerical embellishment. 4B also introduces the "sun," which is seen as analogous to God.

5 which-*comes-out* like-a bridegroom from(+)
his-wedding-canopy,
and like a strong man runs its course with joy.
{It-rejoices as-a-strong-man to-run(+)a-course.} (8/6)

5a   והוא כחתן יצא חפתו

w=6 (x1) [6], hw? 'it, he'=12 (6x2) [12 6x2], k 'as, like' =11 (x1) [20 10x2, 5x4], ḥtn '[bridegroom' =44 (11x4) [458], yṣ? 'comes out' =29 [101], mn 'from' =27 [90 10x9, 6x15, 5x18], ḥph 'wedding canopy' =30 (10x3, 5x6) [93]. Colon totals =159 (not symbolic), and mathematical [780 26x30, 13x60, 10x78, 6x130, 5x156].

The mathematical colon total 780 is highly symbolic with theological factors of 26 for *YHWH*, and 13 (the prime number base of 26), plus 10, 6, and 5, representing the letters of YHW(H). The 10, 6, 5 combination also comes in the alphabetical value of *ḥph*=30 and the mathematical value of *mn*=[90]. A 10–5 combination representing the divine-name YH comes in 5a with the mathematical value of *k*=[20], All of these theological numbers add support for seeing the sun as analogous to YHWH. Also, note that the ambiguous pronoun *hw?* 'it/he' ("it" for "sun", "he" for (God")) begins with the sequence of letters *hw* that comes in the center of *YHWH*, adding to the divine symbolism. This sequence comes only once more in 9Aa with *ṭhwr* 'pure/clean', and the sequence may be a reason, along with the high numerical symbolism, for this unusual adjective describing "fear of the Lord."

5b   ישיש כגבור לרוץ ארח:

śwś 'rejoice' =47 [606 6x101], k 'like' =11 (x1) [20 10x2, 5x4], gbwr 'strong man' =31 [211], l 'to' =12 (6x2) [30 10x3,

5x6], **rwṣ** 'run' =44 (**11**x4) [296], ?rḥ 'course, path'=29 [**209** **11**x19]. The colon totals are **174** (**6**x29) and [**1372** 7x196].

Both cola have mathematical factors of 10, 6, and 5 for YHWH, and of 10 and 5 for YH. Each colon also has both an 11 and a 44 of the alphabetical 22 set. Total cola values for v. 5a+b are 159+174=333 and [780+1372=2152] (both not symbolic).

	Alphabetic		Mathematical	
	Sym. lemmas	Sym. factors	Sym. lemmas	Sym. factors
5a	5/7=71.43%	7/7=100%	4/7=57.14%	7/7=100%
5b	3/6=50%	3/6=50%	4/6=66.67%	7/6=116.67%
5a+b	8/13=61.54%	10/13=76.92%	8/13=61.54%	14/13=107.7%

+

6   Its-rising-is from-the-end-of the-heavens,
    {From-the-*end*-of the-heavens is-its-*going-forth*,}
        {AB: Prep 'end' – Subj}
    and-its-circuit to(=)the-*end-of-them*; (5/6)
        {BA: Subj – Prep 'end'}

   And-nothing is-*hid* from-its-heat. (3)
        {13 letter-line, and alphabetical 'heat'=26}

6Aa   מקצה השמים מוצאו

   mn 'from' =27 [**90** 10x9, **6**x15, **5**x18], qṣh 'end' =42 (**6**x7) [**195** 13x15, **5**x39 (note that 39=26+13)], h=5 (x1) [**5**], šmym 'heavens' =57 [**390** 26x15, 13x30, 10x39, **6**x65, **5**x78], **mwṣh** 'going forth' =42 (**6**x7) [137]. Colon totals =173 [797] (both not symbolic).

"Heavens" makes a beautiful symbolic number inclusio for the first poem, coming in the first colon of the first and last verses. As noted in v. 1 it is highly symbolic with five theological factors including a 26 and the three numbers 10, 6, and 5 for YHW(H), There is only one other lemma in Ps 19 that has five symbolic factors *str* 'hidden' [660=22x30, 11x60, 10x66, 6x110, 5x132]. It comes in the next colon, 6B. As with "heavens," it comes twice, in vv. 6B and also v. 12. This possibly indicates a Wisdom circle's numerological knowledge of the high counts of these two mathematical lemmas prompting their double occurrence in Ps 19.

6Ab   ותקופתו על־קצותם

> **w=6** (x1) [6], tqwph 'circuit' =69 [591], ʕl 'to' =**28** (7x4) [**100** 10x10, 5x20], qṣh 'end' =**42** (6x7) [**195** 13x15, 5x39]. Totals =**145** (5x29) [892]. Totals for 6Aa–b are 173+145=**318** (6x53) and [797+892=1689].

The repetition of *qṣh* 'end' as an inclusio in 6Aa–b is the third doublet after the repeated *ywm* 'day' and *lylh* 'night' in v. 2. Serial repetition is a marker for homogeneous lines leading to a final peak, as in this poem with hexameter lines. The lemma *qṣh* also came in v. 4, with the repetition adding to its significance. The large number of symbolic factors for *qṣh* (6, 7, 13, 5) plus 39, which is significant as 26+13, gives power to it. The alphabetical factors of 6x7 for 42 with *qṣh* also occur with *mwṣh* 'going forth' in 6Aa, adding more numerical parallelism to the parallelism of the inclusio of *qṣh*.

6B   ואין נסתר מחמתו

> **w=6** (x1) [6], ʔyn 'nothing' =**25** (5x5) [61], str 'hid' =57 [**660** 22x30, 11x60, 10x66, 6x110, 5x132], mn 'from' =**27** [**90** 10x9, 6x15, 5x18], ḥmh 'heat' =**26** (x1, 13x2) [53]. Colon totals =**115** (5x23) and [**940** 10x94, 5x188].

This is the final peak of the first poem and is marked with one of the 220% high ratios of symbolic factors by the mathematical count. The last word of the poem, "heat", significantly has the alphabetical value of 26 relating to *YHWH*. As pointed out in 6A, *str* 'hidden' stands out numerically with five symbolic factors 10, 5, and 6 representing the letters YHW(H), and 22 and 11 from the

POEM ONE, 19:1-6

alphabetical set. It significantly comes again in v. 12b, referring to "hidden faults," adding to the extended interpretation in vv. 4-6 of the sun as analogous to God from whom nothing is "hidden."

The total lemma counts for both lines of v. 6 are 318+115=433 [1689+940=**2629** 11x239]. *Mn* [**90**=**10**x9, **6**x15, **5**x18] comes in both 6A and 6B, giving parallelism. It is powerful with the three YHW(H) numbers 10, 6, and 5.

	Alphabetical		Mathematical	
	Sym. lemmas	Sym. factors	Sym lemmas	Sym. factors
6Aa+b	6/9=66.67%	9/9=100%	7/9=77.78%	17/9=188.9%
6B(mon.)	3/5=60%	5/5=100%	3/5=60%	11/5=220%
6A+B	9/14=64.29%	14/14=100%	10/14=71.43%	28/14=200%

Two Tables Analyzing Types of Symbolic Lemmas for the 1st Poem Ps 19:1-6

	Alphabetical		Mathematical	
	Sym. lemmas	Sym. factors	Sym. lemmas	Sym. factors
19:1-6	70/72=97.2%	75/72=104%	94/72=130.6%	96/72=133.3%

The above one-line table has alphabetical ratios compared with mathematical ratios based on the 72 lemmas in 1-6 as the divisor. These figures show that mathematical factors at 133.3% are more numerous than alphabetical factors at 104%. The role in mathematical counts of the 13 letters whose values end in zero adds many to the symbolic factors 10 and 5. The greater number of theological mathematical factors is shown to apply to all of vv. 1-6 in the next table.

	Alphabet.		Mathem.	
(17, 23, 32, 10, 6, 5)	Sym. lem.	Sym. fact.	Sym. lem.	Sym. fac.
Theological (13, 26,^)	x56	x61	x86	x88
Alphabetical (11, 22)	11x6	11x6	11x2	11x2
	22x0	22x0	22x1	22x1
Seven (7)	x8	x8	x5	x5
Ps 19:1–6 Totals	70	75	94	96

Note that a lemma is counted in all three categories of Theological, Alphabet, and Seven if it has symbolic factors in all three, and the totals can be fewer or greater than the 72 lemmas in 19:1–6. The fact that *theological* lemmas are 56 or 80% of the 70 symbolic alphabetical lemma combinations and 86 or 91.5% of the 94 mathematical lemmas is obviously because of the 8 theological numbers listed in parentheses above, compared to only 2 for the alphabet set and 1 for sevens.

The greater totals, 94 and 96, of mathematical counts compared to 70 and 75 of alphabetical counts reflect the role of the 13 letters from *y* to *t* with 10s and 100s in the mathematical symbolic numbers from 10 through 400. This adds a 10 and a 5 factor to all lemma values comprising only any of the last 13 letters. A 5 factor is also added to lemmas comprising only these 13 letters plus an *h*=5. Of the 94 lemma combinations with mathematical theological factors in the first poem, 26 or 27.66% are of this form, with totals of only these 13 letters that end with 0, or that end with 5 if they also have an *h*. These lemmas were likely valued for showing prominence because they have a high number of mathematical factors, as in *mn*=90 and *str*=660 in the final peak in 6B noted above.

Besides the evidence of symbolic lemmas and factors used to enhance the message and structure, note again that the final peak line of the first poem 19:1–6 has 13 letters (half of 26), and that vv. 3 and 4A near the center have 26 letters each, representing *YHWH*.

Poem Two, 19:7–14: Chiasm 555554 4 455555 and a Final Trimeter

(In the following presentation of poem two, the interpretation of the symbolism for the numbers in each line will be minimized and added to the later discussion, "Position in the Clines and Numeric Embellishment in Structure for the 22 Lines.")

7A   The-law-of the-<u>Lord</u> is-perfect,
       reviving the-soul. (5)

7B   The-decrees-of the-<u>Lord</u> are-sure,
       making-wise the-simple. (5)

7Aa   תורת יהוה תמימה

      twrh 'law' =53 [**611** 13x47], **yhwh=26** (x1, 13x2) [**26**x1, **13**x2], tmym 'perfect' =58 [**490** 10x49, 5x98, 7x70]. Colon totals =137 (not symbolic) and mathematical [**1127** 7x161, 23x49].

	Alphabetic		Mathematical	
	Sym. lemmas	Sym. factors	Sym. lemmas	Sym. factors
7Aa	1/3=33.33%	2/3=66.67%	3/3=100%	6/3=200%

     This first colon of the second poem has 200% of mathematical symbolic factors. This group of 200+ high counts begins with 6B and continues through all of v. 7 and on to 8A. The high counts give prominence to the final peak in 6B and the initial three lines of the second poem.

7Ab   משיבת נפש

      šwb 'revive' =29 [**308** 22x14, 11x28, 7x44], **npš** 'soul' =52 (**26**x2, **13**x4) [**430** 10x43 5x86]. Totals =81 (not symbolic) and [**738** 6x123].

	Alphabetic		Mathematical	
	Sym. lemmas	Sym. factors	Sym. lemmas	Sym. factors
7Ab	1/2=50%	2/2=100%	2/2=100%	5/2=250%

Totals for 7A 137+81=218 (not symbolic) and [1127+738=**1865** 5x373].

7Ba עדות יהוה נאמנה

ʕdwt 'decrees' =48 (6*x*8) [480 32x15, 10x48, 6x80, 5x96], yhwh=26 (x1, 13x2) [26x1, 13x2], ʔmn sure' =28 (7x4) [91 13x7]. Totals =102 (**17x6**) [597].

7Bb מחכימת פתי:

ḥkm 'make wise' =32 (x1) [68 17x4], pty 'simple' =49 (7x7) [**490** 10x49, 5x98, 7x70, also note that 49 is 7x7, 98 is 7x14, and 70 is 7x10]. Totals =81 (not symbolic) and [**558** 6x93].

	Alphabetic		Mathematical	
	Sym. lemmas	Sym. factors	Sym. lemmas	Sym. factors
7Ba	3/3=100%	4/3=133.33%	3/3=100%	8/3=266.67%
7Bb	2/2=100%	3/2=150%	2/2=100%	4/2=200%

The line total for 7B is 102+81=183 (not symbolic) [597+558=**1155** 5x231, 11x105, 7x165].

The total for all of 7 is 218+183=401 (not symbolic) [1865+1155=**3120** 26x120, 13x240, 10x312, 6x520, 5x624]. This mathematical verse total of 3,120 is the highest in Psalm 19 and is an amazing theological number. It has the main divine-name number 26 for *YHWH*, its prime number base of 13, and 10, 6, and 5, the three letters of YHW(H). Of the 7 alphabetical symbolic lemmas in v. 7, five are theological and two are with 7s. By

POEM TWO, 19:7-14

mathematical counts, all lemmas, the v. 7 total, and three of the four colon totals are symbolic.

	Alphabetic		Mathematical	
	Sym. lemm.	Sym. factors	Sym. lemmas	Sym. factors
7Aa+b	2/5=40%	4/5=80%	5/5=100%	11/5=220%
7Ba+b	5/5=100%	7/5=140%	5/5=100%	12/5=240%
7A+B	7/10=70%	11/10=110%	10/10=100%	23/10=230%

As noted above in the introduction, the only alphabetical symbolic lemma in 7Aa is $YHWH$=26, and the only one in 7Ab is its numeric double *npš* 'soul'=52 (26x2). All other alphabetical lemmas and the cola totals are not symbolic. This is a beautiful way to focus on the first of seven $YHWH$, by excluding other than these two symbolic lemmas from the first line of the second poem 7A.

+ (2nd strophe of 7, all with 2 lines)

8   The-precepts-of the-<u>Lord</u> are-right,
        rejoicing(=)the-heart. (4/5)
     The-commandment-of the-<u>Lord</u> is-pure,
        enlightening the-eyes. (5)

8Aa   פקודי יהוה ישר

   pqwdym 'precepts' =69 [**240** 10x24, 6x40, 5x48], **yhwh=26** (x1, **13**x2) [**26**x1, **13**x2], **yšr** 'right'=**51** (17x3) [**510** 17x30, 10x51, 6x85, 5x102]. The colon totals are 146 and [776]; both are not symbolic.

8Ab   משמחי-לב

   śmḥ 'rejoice' =**42** (6x7) [**348** 6x58], **lb** 'heart' =**14** (7x2) [**32**]. Totals =56 (not symbolic) [**380** 10x38, 5x76]. Totals for 8A are 146+56=202 and [776+107=883] (both not symbolic).

8Ba מצות יהוה ברה

    mṣwt 'commandment' =59 [536], **yhwh=26** (x1, 13x2) [26x1, 13x2], **br** 'pure' =22 (22x1, 11x2) [202]. Totals =107 [764] (both not symbolic).

8Bb מאירת עינים:

    ʔwr 'enlighten' =27 [**207** 23x9], ʕyn 'eye' 39 (13x3) [130 **26**x5, **13**x10]. Totals =**66** (**22**x3, **11**x6) [337]. Total for 8B =107+66=173 [764+337=1101] (both not symbolic).

The totals for all of v. 8 are 202+173=**375** (**5**x75) and [776+1101=1877 not symbolic].

	Alphabetic		Mathematical	
	Sym. lemmas	Sym. factors	Sym. lemmas	Sym. factors
8Aa	2/3=66.67%	3/3=100%	3/3=100%	9/3=300%
8Ab	2/2=100%	3/2=150%	2/2=100%	2/2=100%
8Aa+b	4/5=80%	6/5=120%	5/5=100%	11/5=220%
8Ba+b	3/5=60%	5/5=100%	3/5=60%	7/5=140%
8A+B	7/10=70%	11/10=110%	8/10=80%	18/10=180%

The mathematical factor count of 300% in 8Aa is one of the two highest colon percentages along with 12b.

    +

9   The-fear-of the-<u>Lord</u> is-pure,
        enduring forever. (5)
    The-ordinances-of=the-<u>Lord</u> are-true;
        and-righteous altogether. (4)

9Aa יראת יהוה טהורה

    yrʔh 'fear' =**36** (**6**x6) [**216 6**x36, or **6**x**6**x**6**], **yhwh=26** (x1, 13x2) [26x1, 13x2], ṭhwr 'pure' =**40** (**10**x4, **5**x20) [220

POEM TWO, 19:7–14

10x22, 5x44, 11x20] (with 6 factors as *mtwq* 'sweet'). Totals =**102** (**17x6**) and [**462** 6x77, 7x66, 22x21, 11x42].

9Ab   עוֹמֶדֶת לָעַד

ʕ*md* 'endure' =**33** (**11x3**) [**114** 6x19], l 'to' =**12** (**6x2**) [**30** 10x3, 5x6], ʕ*d* 'forever' =**20** (**10x2, 5x4**) [**74**]. Totals =**65** (**5x13**) [**218**].

The totals for 9A are 102+65=167 (not symbolic) [462+218=**680** 17x40, 10x68, 5x136]. The plethora of symbolic numbers in 9A is among the most interesting in Ps 19. See v. 9 below in "Position in the Clines and Numeric Embellishment in Structure for the 22 Lines."

9Ba   מִשְׁפְּטֵי־יְהוָה אֱמֶת

mšpṭ 'ordinances' =**60** (**10x6, 5x12**) [**429** 13x33, 11x39 (note that 39=26+13)], *yhwh*=**26** (x1, **13x2**) [**26**x1, **13x2**], ʔ*mt* 'true' =**36** (**6x6**) [**441** 7x63]. Totals =**122** (not symbolic) and [**896** 3 2x28, 7x128]. *Mšpṭ* has the 10, 6, and 5 factors of YHW(H) also found in *pqwdym* 'precepts' in 8Aa.

9Bb   צָדְקוּ יַחְדָּו׃

ṣ*dq* 'righteous' =**41** [**194**], *yḥdw* 'altogether' =**28** (**7x4**) [**98** 7x14]. Totals =**69** (**23x3**), [**292**] (not symbolic).

The totals for v. 9B are alphabetical 122+69=191 (not symbolic), and mathematical [896+292=**1188** 22x54, 11x108, 6x198].

The total for all of v. 9 is alphabetical 167+122=**289** (**17x17**) and mathematical 680+1188=1868 (not symbolic). The short count 17 for *YHWH* is beautifully represented by the total alphabetical count 289=17x17. The mathematical total for 9A of 680 also has a 17, and a 40 showing fullness. Of the ten alphabetical symbolic lemmas in v. 9, eight are theological, and seven of nine are theological by mathematical counts.

	Alphabetic		Mathematical	
	Sym. lemm.	Sym. factors	Sym. lemmas	Sym. factors
9Aa+b	6/6=100%	10/6=166.67%	5/6=83.33%	10/6=166.67%
9Ba+b	4/5=80%	8/5=160%	3/5=60%	6/5=120%
9A+B	10/11=90.9%	18/11=163.6%	8/11=72.73%	16/11=145.5%

+ (Peak strophe, with 3 strophes on each side)

10   More-to-be-desired-are-they than-gold,
even much fine gold;
{They-are-desired more-*than*-gold,
{Central Peak} {repetition of *mn* 'than'}
even-*than*-much fine-gold,} (4)
{10A 17 letters, the short count for *YHWH*}

sweeter-also than-honey
   {10Ba also in Ps 119:103 for "your words"}
and-drippings-of the-honeycomb. (4)

10Aa הנחמדים מזהב

h=5 (x1) [5], ḥmd 'desire'=25 (5x5) [52 26x2, 13x4], mn 'than' =27 [90 10x9, 6x15, 5x18], zhb 'gold' =14 (7x2) [14 7x2]. Totals =71 (not symbolic) and [161 23x7].

10Ab וּמִפַּז רָב

w=6 (x1) [6], mn 'than' =27 [90 10x9, 6x15, 5x18], pz 'fine gold' =26 (x1, 13x2) [87], rb 'much' =22 (x1, 11x2) [202]. Totals =81 (not symbolic) and [385 5x77, 11x35, 7x55].

The totals for 10A are 71+81=152 (not symbolic) [161+385=**546** 26x21, 13x42, 6x91, 7x78, (also note 39x14=546 with 39=26+13)]. Note that the numerical parallelism with *pz* 'fine gold' in 10Ab has the highest symbolic alphabetical value of *YHWH*=26, and in 10Aa the mathematical count of ḥmd 'desired' has the value of 52 or 26x2, plus two alphabetical 5s. The lemma *mn* 'than' (comparative) adds to this numerical parallelism by coming in both cola with the mathematical factors of 10, 5, and 6, the letters of *YHW(H)*.

The lemma *zhb* 'gold,' which forms a word-pair with *pz* 'fine gold,' has the fullness/perfection factor of 7 for both the alphabetical and mathematical counts. The mathematical total of 10Aa has the divine-name number 23 plus a 7, and 10Ab has 385 with another 7 plus an 11 and a 5x77. The many sevens serve nicely as markers for the well-formed peak line of the second poem, and the abundance of symbolic numbers gives it further prominence.

10Ba ומתוקים מדבש

> **w=6** (x1) [**6**], **mtwq** 'sweet'=**60** (**10x6**) [**546 26x21**, **13x42**, **6x91**, **7x78**, (also note 39x14=546 with 39=26+13)], mn 'than' =**27** [**90 10x9**, **6x15**, **5x18**], dbš 'honey' =**27** [**306 17x18**]. Totals =**120** (**10x12**, **5x24**) and [**948 6x158**].

10Bb ונפת צופים

> **w=6** (x1) [**6**], **npt** 'drip' =**52** (**26x2**, **13x4**) [**530 10x53**, **5x106**], ṣwp 'honeycomb' =**41** [**176 22x8**, **11x16**]. Totals =**99** (**11x9**), [712].

Totals for 10B: 120+99=219 (not symbolic) [948+712=**1660** **10x166**, **5x332**].

Totals for all of v. 10: 152+219=**371** (**7x53**) [546+1660=2206 not symbolic]. Of the 9 alphabetical symbolic lemmas, 8 are in the theological set. Of the 12 mathematical symbolic lemmas, 10 are theological.

	Alphabetic		Mathematical	
	Sym. lemm.	Sym. factors	Sym lemmas	Sym. factors
10Aa+b	4/8=57.14%	9/8 = 112.5%	6/8 = 75%	11/8=137.5%
10Ba+b	4/7=57.14%	6/7 = 85.71%	7/7=100%	14/7=200%
10A+B	8/15=53.3%	15/15=100%	13/15=86.7%	25/15=166.7%

++ (2nd Stanza of 2nd Poem, with 3 strophes of 2 lines each)

11 Moreover=by-them is-your-servant warned;
in-keeping-them there-is-great(+)reward. (6/5)

11a גם־עבדך נזהר בהם

gm 'moreover' =16 [43], ʿbd 'servant' =22 (x1, 11x2) [76], zhr 'warned' =32 (x1) [212], b 'by' =2 [2]. Totals =72 (6x12), [333]. (Note: This is the only colon with no mathematical symbolic numbers.)

11b בשמרם עקב רב:

b 'in' =2 [2], šmr 'keep, obey' =54 (6x9) [540 10x54, 6x90, 5x108], ʿqb 'reward' =37 [172], rb 'great' =22 (x1, 11x2) [202]. Totals =115 (5x23), [916]. (Note that the only mathematical symbolic number in v. 11 is with the lemma šmr 'keeping.' This highlights the message of "keeping" God's ordinances.)

The totals for v. 11a–b are 72+115=**187** (**17x11**) and [333+916=1249 not symbolic]. The factors for the alphabetical total 187 are significant as 17 is the short count for YHWH, and 11 is the base of the 22-set.

POEM TWO, 19:7-14

	Alphabetic		Mathematical	
	Sym. lemmas	Sym. factors	Sym. lemmas	Sym. factors
11a	2/4=50%	3/4=75%	0/4= 0%	0/4=0%
11b	2/4=50%	3/4=75%	1/4=25%	3/4=75%
11a+b	4/8=50%	6/8=75%	1/8=12.5%	3/8=37.5%

12   Who(=)can-detect their-errors?
     Clear-me from-<u>hidden</u>-faults. (4/5)

12a   שגיאות מי־יבין

šgyʔh 'error' =**40** (**10**x**4**, **5**x**8**) [**319** **11**x**29**], **my** 'who' =**23** (x**1**) [**50** **10**x**5**], **byn** 'detect, understand, =**26** (x**1**, **13**x**2**) [**62**]. Totals =**89**, [**431**] (both not symbolic).

12b   מנסתרות נקני:

mn 'from' = **27** [**90** **10**x**9**, **6**x**15**, **5**x**18**], **str** 'hide' =**57** [**660** **22**x**30**, **11**x**60**, **10**x**66**, **6**x**110**, **5**x**132**], **nqh** 'clear, empty' =**38** [**155** **5**x**35**]. Totals =**122** (not symbolic) and [**905** **5**x**181**]. By alphabetical counts, none of the three lemmas nor the colon total is symbolic, making 12b the lowest colon in the psalm at 0% for both alphabetical lemmas and factors.

Totals for 12 are 89+122=211 and [431+905=1336] (both not symbolic).

	Alphabetic		Mathematical	
	Sym. lemmas	Sym. factors	Sym. lemmas	Sym. factors
12a	3/3=100%	5/3=166.67%	2/3=66.67%	3/3=100%
12b	0/3=0%	0/3=0%	3/3=100%	9/3=300%
12a+b	3/6=50%	5/6=83.33%	5/6=83.33%	12/6=200%

+

13   Keep-back(+)your-servant also from-the-insolent
{RSV presumptuous sins};
{Hebrew word order: Also from-presumptuous
(GNT wilful)-sins keep-back(+)your-servant;}
do-not(=)let-them-have-dominion=over-me. (5)
Then I-shall-be-blameless and-innocent
of-{Hebrew 'from'}-great transgression. (5)

13Aa גם מזדים חשך עבדך

gm 'also' =16 [43], mn 'from' =27 [90 10x9, 5x18, 6x15], zd 'wilful sins' =11 (x1) [11], ḥśk 'keep back' =40 (10x4, 5x8) [328], ʕbd 'servant' =22 (22x1, 11x2) [76]. Totals =116, [548] (both not symbolic).

13Ab אל־ימשלו־בי

ʔl 'not' =13 (x1) [31], mšl 'rule' =46 (23x2) [370 10x37, 5x74], b 'over' =2 [2]. Totals =61 (not symbolic), [403 13x31].

Totals for 13A: alphabetical 116+61=177, mathematical [548+403=951] (both not symbolic).

13Ba אז איתם ונקיתי

ʔz 'then' =8 [8], **tmm** 'blameless' =48 (6x8) [480 32x15, 10x48, 6x80, 5x96], w 'and' =6 (x1) [6], nqh 'clear,

POEM TWO, 19:7-14

innocent'=38 [**155** 5x31]. Totals =109 (not symbolic), [**649** 11x59].

13Bb: מפשע רב

mn 'from' =27 [**90** 10x9, **6**x15, **5**x18], pšʿ 'transgression' =**54** (6x9) [**450** 10x45 6x75, 5x90], **rb** 'great' =**22** (x1, 11x2) [202]. Totals =**100** (**10x10**, **5**x20), [**742** 7x106].

Totals for 13B: alphabetical 109+100=209 (**11**x19), mathematical [649+742=**1391** 13x107].

The totals for v. 13 are 177+109=386 and [951+1391= 2302] (both not symbolic).

	Alphabetic		Mathematical	
	Sym. lemmas	Sym. factors	Sym. lemmas	Sym. factors
13Aa+b	5/8=62.5%	7/8=87.5%	3/8=37.5%	6/8=75%
13Ba+b	4/7=57.14%	5/7=71.43%	5/7=71.43%	12/7=171.43%
13A+B	9/15=60%	12/15=80%	8/15=53.33%	18/15=120%

+

14 Let the words of my mouth and the meditation of my heart be acceptable to you,
{Let the-words-of=my-mouth be-acceptable}
{AB: Prep *l* Gen+N//}
   {and-the-meditation-of(+)my-heart before-you,} (6/5)
   {BA: Gen+N Prep *l*}

14B O-<u>Lord</u>, my-rock and-my-redeemer. (3)
{Lord the 7th time}

14Aa יהיו לרצון אמרי־פי

> hyh 'be' =20 (10x2, 5x4) [20 10x2, 5x4], l 'for' =12 (6x2) [30 10x3, 5x6], rṣwn 'acceptable' =58 [346], ʔmr 'word' =34 (17x2) [241], ph 'mouth' =22 (x1, 11x2) [85 17x5]. Totals =146 [722] (both not symbolic).

14Ab והגיון לבי לפניך

> w=6 (x1) [6], hgywn 'meditation' =38 [74], lb 'heart' =14 (7x2) [32], l 'to' =12 (6x2) [30 10x3, 5x6], pnh 'face' =36 (6x6) [135 5x27]. Totals =106 [277] (both not symbolic).

The totals for 14A are alphabetic 146+106=252 (6x42, 7x36), and mathematical [722+277=999].

14B יהוה צורי וגאלי:

> yhwh=26 (x1, 13x2) [26x1, 13x2], ṣwr 'rock' =44 (22x2, 11x4) [296], w=6 (x1) [6], gʔl 'redeemer' =16 [34 17x2]. Totals =92 (23x4), [362] (not symbolic).

The totals for v. 14 are alphabetical lemma counts 252+92=344, and mathematical 999+362=1361 (both not symbolic). Of the 11 alphabetical symbolic lemmas in 14A–B, 8 are in the theological set, and in the mathematical set, all 10 are theological.

	Alphabetical		Mathematical	
	Sym. lemmas	Sym. factors	Sym. lemmas	Sym. factors
14Aa+b	8/10=80%	11/10=110%	7/10=70%	14/10=130%
14B(m.)	3/4=75%	5/4=125%	3/4=75%	4/4=100%
14A+B	11/14=78.57%	16/14=114.2%	10/14=71.4%	18/14=128.6%

TABLE 1: TYPES OF SYMBOLIC FACTORS

Table 1: Types of Symbolic Factors in poems Ps 19:1–6 and 7–14, and Total 1–14

In both sections of the following table, factors are counted by the three categories of theological, alphabet 22, and seven. Note the high counts in both tables for the basic YHWH number 26 and for its prime number base 13, compared to the other divine-name numbers 17, 23, and 32.

	Poem 1 19:1–6		Poem 2 19:7–14	
	Alphabetical	Mathema.	Alphabetical	Mathem.
Type	Sym. fact.	Sym. fac.	Sym. fact.	Sym. fac.
Theological 13,	x9	x6	x13	x12
26,	x2	x4	x11	x10
17,	x3	x2	x2	x5
23,	x2	x1	x4	x1
32,	x1	x2	x2	x5
10,	x3	x20	x7	x25
6,	x23	x24	x23	x25
5	x61	x88	x10	x32
Theol. Totals	104	147	72	115
Alphabet 11,	x9	x8	x9	x8
22	x8	x4	x8	x4
Seven (7)	x8	x11	x8	x11
Totals	129	170	97	138

Poems 1–2 Total		Sym Factors	19:1–14
		Alphabetical	Mathematical
Theological	13,	x22	x18
	26,	x13	x14
	17,	x5	x7
	23,	x6	x2
	32,	x3	x7
	10,	x10	x45
	6,	x46	x49
	5	x71	x120
Theol. Totals		176	257
Alphabet	11,	x18	x16
	22	x16	x8
Seven (7)		x16	x22
Ps 19 Totals		226	308

In the above "Poems 1–2 Total" list, the YHW(H) number 6 shows a greater number of 46 hits with alphabetical factors than 10, which has only 10. This comes from ten conjunctions $w=6$, and from the greater number of hits possible with a smaller divisor. The mathematical count for 10 is 45, and 6 is 49, with 6 getting 10 hits from the conjunction w. The highest number of 145 mathematical hits for factors of 5 includes 43 ending with zero and five $h=5$ articles. Five for articles is only 4% of the 123 words in the poetic 1–14. A reduction of articles in poetry is typical of Hebrew poetry. Bekins notes 9% for standard prose in Genesis, and 6% for high-count psalms that are mainly dated late.[24] The first colon 1a, and first peak colon 10Aa, as well as the first colon of the 26-letter 4Aa, all have $h=5$ articles and significant mathematical symbolic factors, which may indicate adding articles was one way colon totals were adjusted. Bevin notes, "Most candidates for omission occur with globally unique referents".[25] "Heavens" in 19:1a is a

---

24. Bekins ("The Omission of the Definite Article," 4–6).
25. Bekins ("The Omission of the Definite Article," 9).

"globally unique referent." Note the "omission" in Ps 50.6 "heavens declare his righteousness" without the article h on "heavens" in contrast to 19:1a "The heavens are telling the glory of God" with h and a colon total of alphabetical 150 (10x15, 6x25, 5x30) and mathematical 798 [7x114, 6x133]. If h=5 is deleted, there are only 2 factors instead of 5 in the colon total—145 (5x29) and 793 [13x61]. "Firmament" also has a definite article in the next colon 1b. Both of these are "globally unique referents," which are definite by their nature, and the article is redundantly added.

The peak line 10Aa of the second poem also has an h=5 and has a mathematical symbolic colon total of 161 with factors of a divine-name number 23 and fullness 7. There are 8 symbolic factors in the total of the two cola and line. If the h=5 were not there, it would be only one less with 7. Bekins notes that this combination of h with a participle is a "semi-relative construction" and is less likely to be deleted than other articles.[26]

The first colon of the 26-letter 4A also has an h=5 and a mathematical total of 207 with a divine-name factor of 23. The article comes with all occurrences of "all the earth" in at least Genesis and Psalms, so it is a stereotype and not a candidate for deletion. The colon also has a preposition b=2, helping to make the 207. The second colon of the 13-letter line 4A also has a b, and has a mathematical total of 710 with factors of 10x5 equivalent to YH. The introductory line 4B of the second stanza of the first poem, which introduces the sun, also has a b and has an alphabetical 121 with 11x11, and a mathematical 1058 with 23x46. The divine name 23 is further enhanced by 46=23+23. Note that 23 also comes in 4A and the peak line 10A of the second poem. The second colon 11b of the second stanza of the second poem also has a b, and an alphabetical total of 115 with 23x5. The first colon 11a also has a b and a total of 72 with 6x12 with 12=6+6. One more b comes in the penultimate 13Ab with a colon total of 403 (13x31) with the

---

26. Bekins ("The Omission of the Definite Article," 19). Bekins explains that the tendency not to delete the h of semi-relative constructions is because they retain an older demonstrative function rather than being markers of definiteness.

base 13 of the 26-set. This list is impressive since all five *b*'s in Ps 19 have a symbolic number in their colon total, which could have been facilitated by arranging the sentence to include a *b* in the cola if the other lemmas were short by two.

In 19:1a there are a few manuscripts where the MT lemma *mʕśh* 'work' =55 (5x11) [415 5x83] has a final *y*=10 instead of *h*=5. This occurs elsewhere, for example, in the genitive *mʕśy* in Jer 1:16, which also has the noun "hands." The value of *mʕśy* is 60 (10x6, 5x15) [420 10x42, 7x60, 5x84], significantly increasing symbolic factors from three to six. Colon totals in 19:1 had no symbolic factors with *mʕśh*, but with *mʕśy* the mathematical total is 882 with 6x147 and 7x126. The v. 1 mathematical totals also increase from one to three with *mʕśh*=1675 5x335, but *mʕśy*=5x336, 6x280, and 7x240. It is reasonable to expect that a poet attuned to symbolic numbers would choose the higher-valued form for important places like v. 1 when given a spelling difference with such a big symbolic difference. This could account for and give support to the *mʕśy* textual variant.

Lemmas with two identical factors, such as 6x6 or 7x7, are especially powerful symbolically. The mathematical value for *ʕl* 'to', which is 100 or 10x10, comes in 6A, the colon before the final peak line of the first poem. The 100 could anticipate the poem's completion, especially since the noun connected to it is *qsh* 'end', the last word of the line, which is also the first word in an inclusio for 6A. The doublet 49=7x7, suggesting perfection, comes with the alphabetic count of *pty* 'simple' in 7Bb, the final colon of the first verse of the Torah poem. The two 26-letter lines vv. 3 and 4A have two alphabetical lemmas each with doublets. They are *ʔyn* 'no' twice in 3a, *qw* 'line' in 4Aa, all with the value of 25=5x5, and *tbl* 'world' in 4Ab with 36=6x6. They form a buildup to the secondary peak in 4B with *ʔhl* 'tent' having three factors of 6— alphabetical 18=6x3 and mathematical 36=6x6. These doublets numerically connect the two 26-letter lines 3 and 4A to the short secondary peak 4B, which is the first line of the second stanza. There are three more alphabetical lemmas in Ps 19 with 36=6x6. *Yrʔh* 'fear in 9A, which is exceptional since "fear of the Lord"

TABLE 2: CLINE OF ALPHABETICAL NUMBERS

does not come in Ps 119, is numerically loaded with alphabetical 36=6x6 plus mathematical 216=6x36, or 6x6x6. The other two with alphabetical 36=6x6 are *ʔmt* 'true' in 9Ba and *pnh* 'face' in 14Ab, which is the last word before the final secondary peak 14B. The colon total for 9Ba is interesting with mathematical double digits 462=6x77, 7x66, 22x21, and 11x42, plus alphabetical 102=17x6. 9B is the line before the central peak 10A, so the numerical plethora may be introducing the peak.

Four Tables of Clines of Symbolic Lemmas and Symbolic Factors in Ps 19

In the following Tables 2, 3, 4, and 5, the two left-hand columns show the percentage of symbolic *lemmas* divided by the number of lemmas in each poetic line. The two right-hand columns show the percentage of all symbolic *factors* in each line divided by the lemma total for the line. In the factor column, multiple symbolic factors in any lemma's value are all counted to give credit to the greater symbolism for lemmas with multiple symbolic factors. If two or more verses or lines have the same percentage, they are listed with consecutive rather than repeated ordinals, as with the 1st and 2nd 100% lemmas below. In discussing their order, they are considered tied for 1st.

Table 2: Cline of Ratios of *Alphabetical* Number Symbolism by Poetic Lines

% of Symbolic Lemmas by Lines		% of Symbolic Factors by Lines	
100% (1st-2nd)	7B 1st	166.67%	9A 1st
100% (1st-2nd)	9A 2nd	160%	9B 2nd
90.91%	v. 1 3rd	140%	7B 3rd
87.5%	v. 3 4th	137.5%	v. 3 4th
80% (5th-8th)	9B 5th	125%	14B 5th

% of Symbolic Lemmas by Lines		% of Symbolic Factors by Lines	
80% (5th-8th)	14A 6th	120%	8A 6th
80% (5th-8th)	8A 7th	118.18% (7th-8th)	v. 1 7th
80% (5th-8th)	8B 8th	118.18% (7th-8th)	4A 8th
76.92%	v. 5 9th	112.5% (9th-10th)	4B 9th
75% (10th-11th)	4B 10th	112.5% (9th-10th)	10A 10th
75% (10th-11th)	14B 11th	110% (11th-12th)	8B 11th
72.73% (12th-13th)	4A 12th	110% (11th-12th)	14A 12th
72.73% (12th-13th)	v. 2 13th	100%	6B 13th
66.67%	6B 14th	90.91%	6A 14th
63.64%	6A 15th	87.5%	13A 15th
62.5%	13A 16th	85.71%	10B 16th
57.14% (17th-19th)	10A 17th	83.33%	v. 12 17th
57.14% (17th-19th)	10B 18th	80%	7A 18th
57.14% (17th-19th)	13B 19th	75%	v. 11 19th
50% (20th-21st)	v. 12 20th	73.33%	v. 5 20th
50% (20th-21st)	v. 11 21st	72.73%	v. 2 21st
40%	7A 22nd	71.43%	13B 22nd

Verses 9A, 7B, and v. 1 are at the top of the alphabetical cline in Table 2. As proposed above, 9A has a special focus because of the subject "the fear of the Lord," which is the only subject in the series in vv. 7–9 not found in Ps 119. V. 1 is structurally important as the first poetic line of Ps 19, and the high count enhances its prominence. The first verse of the second poem, v. 7, is unique—on the one hand 7B is tied as highest along with 9A for alphabetical lemmas, but on the other hand, 7A has the lowest 22nd for lemmas, and 18th for factors. As noted above, the low counts are because only $YHWH=26$ in 7Aa and $npš=52$ or $26×2$ in 7Ab are symbolic, bringing the 7A alphabetical ratios down to 40% for lemmas and

TABLE 3: CLINE OF MATHEMATICAL NUMBERS

80% for factors. 7B follows as highest by symbolic lemmas, and in 3rd place by factors. V. 7 thereby highlights the beginning of the cluster of high ratios that continues to 8A, having the 6th highest place by factors. Also in Table 2, v. 3 comes 4th in both columns and is significant as having 26 letters, as does the next v. 4A. The very low 21st place for factors in v. 2 serves to set off the higher 7th place for v. 1, as does the lemma differences of 12th place for v. 2 and 3rd place for v. 1.

Table 3: Cline of Ratios of *Mathematical* Number Symbolism by Poetic Lines

% of Symbolic Lemmas by Lines		% of Symbolic Factors by Lines	
100% (1st-5th)	7B 1st	240%	7B 1st
100% (1st-5th)	7A 2nd	220% (2nd-5th)	7A 2nd
100% (1st-5th)	8A 3rd	220% (2nd-5th)	8A 3rd
100% (1st-5th)	10B 4th	220% (2nd-5th)	6B 4th
100% (1st-5th)	14B 5th	220% (2nd-5th)	4B 5th
83.33% (6th-7th)	v. 12 6th	200% (6th-7th)	10B 6th
83.33% (6th-7th)	9A 7th	200% (6th-7th)	v. 12 7th
81.82%	v. 1 8th	171.43%	13B 8th
80%	4B 9th	166.67%	9A 9th
75%	10A 10th	154.55%	6A 10th
72.73%	v. 2 11th	145.45%	v. 1 11th
71.43%	13B 12th	140%	8B 12th
70%	14A 13th	137.5%	10A 13th
66.67% (14th-15th)	v. 5 14th	130%	14A 14th
66.67% (14th-15th)	6B 15th	120%	9B 15th
63.64%	6A 16th	109.09%	v. 2 16th
60% (17th-18th)	8B 17th	107.69%	v. 5 17th

45

% of Symbolic Lemmas by Lines		% of Symbolic Factors by Lines	
60% (17th-18th)	9B 18th	100%	14B 18th
54.54%	4A 19th	75% (19th-20th)	13A 19th
50%*	v. 3 20th	75%* (19th-20th)	v.3 20th
37.5%	13A 21st	72.73%	4A 21st
12.5%	v. 11 22nd	37.5%	v. 11 22nd

(* Note that *colon* 3a has only 20% for both lemmas and factors. Colon 3b has 100% and 166.67%, giving the above 50% and 75%.)

The above Table 3 of mathematical symbolic numbers is striking in that the first three lines of the Torah poem are all among the highest, giving them special prominence. The highest is 7B with 12 factors divided by 5 lemmas, or 240%, and 7A and 8A have 220% with 11 factors divided by 5 lemmas. Since YHWH with 2 factors is common in all three lines, the requirement for an author to produce this would be to incorporate other lemmas in each of the first three lines so that there would be a total of 11 or more mathematical factors in each line. 7A has *twrh* with 1, *YHWH* with 2, *tmym* with 3, *swab* with 3, and *npš* with 2, totaling 11. 7B has *ʕdwt* with 4, *YHWH* with 2, *ʔmn* with 2, *ḥkm* with 1, and pty with 3, totaling 12. And 8A has *pqwdym* with 3 factors, *YHWH* with 2, *yšr* with 4, *śmḥ* with 1, and *lb* with 1, totaling 11. What is the literary significance of this? I see it as very strong evidence that the author purposefully chose lemmas with a high number of factors to enhance these first three lines 7A, 7B, and 8A of the Torah poem in Ps 19:7–14.

As noted in Table 2, *alphabetical* 7A has the lowest percentage with only one symbolic word in each colon—*YHWH*=26 and *npš* 'soul'=52 (26x2)—and is listed at the bottom (22nd) of Table 2 with only 33.33% symbolic. Alphabetical 7B, however, is similar to the above mathematical counts with the same highest percentage of 100% for lemmas, and third place 140% for factors. All five lemmas in 7B are symbolic in both alphabetical and mathematical counts, giving 100% in symbolic lemmas in both Tables 2 and 3.

TABLE 4: MATHEMATICAL NUMBERS PLUS COLA TOTALS

Clines Including Cola Totals for Symbolic Lemmas and Factors

Total counts of lemmas and factors in cola and lines have been shown in the line-by-line analysis above to contain significant symbolic numbers and factors. For example, the first colon of Ps 19 has 150 with alphabetical factors of 10, 6, and 5, and the first colon 7Aa of the Torah poem has a mathematical total of 490 with factors of 10, 5, and 7. Can a cline in a table show that cola totals contribute to the numerical structure of the psalm? The next two Tables 4 and 5, would say "Yes." They differ from the above Tables 2 and 3 by adding the number of cola of each line to the divisors, and the number of symbolic lemmas or factors in the cola totals to the dividends. The following Table 4 lists the ratios of mathematical symbolic lemmas and factors plus cola totals, divided by the total number of lemmas plus cola totals for each of the 22 poetic lines. Significant results will be discussed after each table.

Table 4: Cline of Mathematical Counts of Lemmas and Factors Plus Cola Totals

Symbolic Lemmas Plus Cola Totals		Symbolic Factors Plus Cola Totals	
7/7=100%	7A 1st	13/6=216.67%	6B 1st
8/9=88.89%	10B 2nd	15/7=214%	7A 2nd
6/7=85.71%	7B (3rd-4th) 3rd	12/6=200%	4B 3rd
6/7=85.71%	8A (3rd-4th) 4th	13/7=185.71%	7B (4rd-5th) 4th
11/13=84.62%	v. 1 5th	13/7=185.71%	8A (4rd-5th) 5th
5/6=83.33%	4B (monoc.) 6th	15/9=166.67%	10B 6th
8/10=80%	10A (7th-8th) 7th	16/10=160%	10A 7th
4/5=80%	14B (mc.) (7th-8th) 8th	14/9=155.56%	13B 8th
7/9=77.78%	13B 9th	17/11–154.6%	6A 9th
9/12=75%	v. 2 (10th-12th) 10th	12/8=150%	9A 10th

SWEETER THAN HONEY

Symbolic Lemmas Plus Cola Totals		Symbolic Factors Plus Cola Totals	
6/8=75%	9A (10th-12th) 11th	13/8=144.44%	v. 12a-b 11th
6/8=75%(a=50)	v. 12 (10th-12th) 12th	18/13=138.5%	v. 1 12th
4/6=66.67%	6B (mc.) (13-14th) 13th	20/15=133.3%	v. 5 13th
10/15=66.67%	v. 5 (13th-14th) 14th	14/12=116.7%	v. 2 (14-15th) 14th
7/1=63.64%	6A 15th	14/12=116.7%	14A (14-15th) 15th
8/13=61.54%	4A 16th	8/7=114.29%	9B 16th
7/12=58.33%	14Aa-b 17th	11/11=100%	4A (17th-18th) 17th
4/7=57.14%	9B 18th	7/7=100%	8B (17th-18th) 18th
5/10=50%	v. 3 19th	9/10=90%	v. 3 19th
3/7=42.86%	8B 20th	4/5=80%	14B 20th
4/10=40%	13A 21st	7/10=70%	13A 21st
2/10=20% lowest	v. 11 (a*=0) 22nd	5/10=50% lwst.	v. 11 (a 0%) 22nd

(*Note that 11a is the lowest mathematical *colon* with no symbolic lemmas, although 11b has lemmas at 40% and factors at 100%, giving 20% and 50% for the line.)

The above right-hand mathematical counts of factors in lines significantly have the five highest ratios on 6B, the final peak of the first poem, on 7A, 7B, and 8A the first three lines of the second poem, and on 4B the first line of the second stanza of the first poem. The sixth highest is 10B, the second line in v. 10 after the peak 10A, which is the seventh highest. These all significantly show greater numerical marking in *structural high points* of Ps 19. In the left-hand *lemma* columns, 7A is 1st, and 7B and 8A are tied for 3rd, showing a similar ranking for the first two lines of the second poem. 10B is 2nd, adding to the marking of the central verse, which includes the peak of the second poem, 10A, which is 7th in the lemma cline.

The lowest ratios in the above clines are also interesting. V. 11 has the lowest percentages of all 22 lines for mathematical lemmas and factors in both Table 3 (12.5% and 37.5%) and Table 4 (20% and 50%). This is because it has no symbolic mathematical numbers in 11a, and 11b has only one lemma, *šmr* 'keep'. Having only one mathematical symbolic lemma in the verse highlights that lemma. It emphasizes the importance of *keeping* "the ordinances of the Lord," the subject introduced in 9B. 9A has the unique "fear of the Lord," and 11A has "by them is your servant warned," which both point to the seriousness of guarding one's relationship and reverence for God.[27] The peak of the poem comes in v. 10 between these admonitions, positively comparing God's ordinances to "gold" and "honey."

There are two other places where low ratios set off high ratios. In mathematical Table 4, the cluster of high ratios in 6B through 8A ends abruptly with 8B having the 20th place out of 22 in lemma ratios and 17th for factors. Table 5 also has 8B ranked at 20th for lemmas, and 19th for factors. 9A is average, but 9B is also low, with lemmas at 18% and factors at 16%. These low counts after the high counts at the juncture of the poems make the high counts more pronounced.

The other place with significantly low counts is at the end of Ps 19, where in Table 4 v. 13A comes 21st for both lemmas and factors, and 14A comes 17th and 13th. In contrast, the final colon 14B "O Lord, my rock and my redeemer" is higher in symbolic lemmas and comes 7th in Table 4 and 5th in Table 3. This difference is even stronger in Table 5, which follows below—14B is 3rd for factors, and is 5th for lemmas. In the other alphabetical Table 2, 14B is 5th for factors and 11th for lemmas. 14B, as the final secondary peak of Ps 19, is marked by having significantly higher counts than the lines preceding it.

Some significant structural high points have better numerically symbolic ratios of lemmas and factors when cola totals are counted. For example, the mathematical count for factors in 6B,

---

27. There is another example of isolating lemmas for emphasis in 7A the first line of the second poem. As noted above, each colon has only one symbolic lemma—7Aa with YHWH= 26, and 7Ab with alphabetical *npš* 'soul'= 52 or 2x26. This numerical strategy highlights these two keywords.

the final peak of the first poem, which is ranked 1st in Table 4 with cola totals, but 13th in alphabetical Table 2 without cola totals. Similarly, the mathematical count for lemmas in the peak 10A is 7th at 80% in Table 4 with cola totals, but 10th at 75% in Table 3 without them. Besides high rankings in the tables, the actual symbolic numbers of some cola totals look like numerical enhancement, especially in structural and thematic high points. Note: (1) *150* with alphabetical factors 10, 6, and 5 in 1a the first colon of Ps 19, (2) *1,058* with mathematical factors of 23x46 (and 46=23+23) in the secondary peak 4B, (3) *780* with 26, 13, 10, 6, and 5 in 5a supporting an analogy between the sun and God, (4) *940* with 10 and 5 in the peak 6B, and (5) *462* with mathematical factors 6x77, 7x66, 22x21, 11x42 in the colon 9Aa with "fear of the Lord." The places where counting cola totals gives a better correlation between high points and a greater use of symbolic numbers support the proposal that cola totals should be added to lemma and factor totals for numerical analysis. This is not a claim that authors normally added up lemma values in all cola, but that their motivation for marking literary and thematic high points with symbolic numbers included an awareness that cola totals carry symbolic potential. The greater cola numbers in strategic places support considering that at least some of these significant cola totals were not by chance.

Table 5: Cline of Alphabetic Counts of Lemmas and Factors Plus Cola Totals

Symbolic Lemmas Plus Cola Totals		Symbolic Factors Plus Cola Totals	
8/8=100%	9A 1st	14/8=175%	9A 1st
6/7=85.71%	7B 2nd	9/7=128.57%	7B 2nd
11/13=84.6%	v. 1 3rd	6/5=120%	14B 3rd
5/6=83.33%	4B (monocolon) 4th	7/6=116.67%	6B (monoc.) (4-5) 4th
4/5=80%	14B 5th	7/6=116.67%	4B (monoc.) (4-5) 5th

TABLE 5: ALPHABETIC NUMBERS PLUS COLA TOTALS

Symbolic Lemmas Plus Cola Totals		Symbolic Factors Plus Cola Totals	
7/10=70%	v. 3 6th	15/13=115.4%	v. 1 6th
9/13=69.23%	v. 2 7th	8/7=114.29%	8A (7th-8th) 7th
8/12=66.6%	14A 8th	8/7=114.29%	9B (7th-8th) 8th
7/11=63.6%	6Aa+b 9th	11/10=110%	v. 3 9th
8/13=61.5%	4Aa+b 10th	13/13=100%	4A (10-12th) 10th
9/15=60%	v. 5 11th	10/10=100%	v. 11 (10-12th) 11th
6/10=60%	v. 11 12th	15/15=100%	v. 5 (10-12th) 12th
4/7=57.14%	9B (13th-14th) 13th	11/12=91.67%	14A 13th
4/7=57.14%	v. 12 (13th-14th) 14th	10/11=90.91%	6A 14th
5/9=55.56%	10B (15th-16th) 15th	9/10=90%	10A 15th
5/9=55.56%	13B (15th-16th) 16th	8/9=88.89%	10B 16th
4/7=51.14%	8A 17th	6/7=85.71%	v. 12 17th
3/6=50%	6B (monoc.)(18-19) 18th	7/9=77.78%	13B 18th
5/10=50%	13A (18th-19th) 19th	5/7=71.43%	8B 19th
3/7=42.86%	8B 20th	9/13=69.23%	v. 2 20th
4/10=40%	10A 21st	4/7=57.14%	7A 21st
2/7=28.57%	7A (a 1/4=25%) 22nd	3/10=30%	13A 22nd

The highest counts in Table 5 for alphabetic counts plus cola totals are in v. 9A for both lemmas and factors. In Table 2, which does not count cola totals, 9A was also the highest for lemmas and factors. As noted above, 9A is exceptional in having "fear of the Lord" instead of one of the key terms from Ps 119. The numerous symbolic factors in 9A give it a special numerical significance.

Table 5 has 7B in 2nd place for both lemmas and factors. It also has the final secondary peak 14B in 3rd place for factors and 5th place for lemmas. The beginning line of the second stanza 4B comes 4th in both lemmas and factors. The final peak of the first poem 6B is tied for 4th with factors. Note that all of these are at structural junctures, and 4B and 14B are monocola and therefore are secondary peaks because they break the bicola norm.

On the low end in Table 5, 8B, the first line after the cluster of high ratios at the juncture of the poems from 6B-8A, is near the bottom at 20th for lemmas and 19th for factors. Also, 12b, the colon which begins the low counts before the final secondary peak in 14B, has no symbolic lemmas or factors or 0% in the alphabetical counts. 13A, which continues the low counts, is 22nd or last in Table 5 for alphabetical symbolic factors with 3/10=30%. 13B is also low as 18th with 77.78% for factors, and 14A is 13th with 91.67%. These are all significantly lower than the final peak 14B, which is 3rd for factors and 5th for lemmas in Table 5. Although not as strong as Table 5, Table 2, with alphabetical counts without colon totals, has 7 of the 8 rankings in vv. 12-14A lower than 14B. The higher ranking comes in 14A for factors. Tables 3 and 4 have all four lemma counts for vv. 12-14A lower than the 100% for 14B in Table 3 and 80% in Table 4, although with factors, only 13A is lower than 14B in both tables. These low figures set off the adjacent juncture lines 6B-8A and final secondary peak 14B with their higher ratios.

Position in the Clines and Numeric Embellishment in Structure for the 22 Lines

The data from the above five clines and details from the "Line by Line Analysis" of lemmas and factors will be brought together in the following discussion of structure and numerical prominence in each of the 22 poetic lines.

V. 1 is the third highest for lemmas in both alphabetic Tables 2 and 5. For alphabetical *factors*, Table 5 has v. 1 in 6th place, and Table 2 in 7th place. The fairly high percentages result from four of the five lemmas in the first colon and all six in the second colon being symbolic. The exception is *šmym* 'heavens', which is not symbolic by the alphabetical count, but by the mathematical count is 390 with five theological factors [26, 13, 10, 6, and 5]. The first colon 1a has 10 mathematical symbolic factors in the 5 lemmas, giving 200%. Two other lemmas relating to *YHWH* in v. 1a are *spr* 'tell' with 52 or twice the value of *YHWH*=26, and *?l* 'God' with 13 or half of 26. "God" *?l* (El) is the only divine name in the first poem. The second poem has seven *YHWH*, with the first in its first colon as here.[28] The lemma *tmm* 'perfect' =490 has high mathematical factors 10x49, 5x98, 7x70. Also note that 49 is 7x7, 98 is 7x14, and 70 is 7x10, giving further focus to 7 in each of the three non-symbolic factors. Significantly, *tmm* also comes as the second word in Ps 119, and its first colon 1a also has 6 factors for 3 lemmas or 200% for mathematical factors. This is the same ratio as Ps 19:1a. *Tmm* comes again in Ps 119:80. It also comes in Ps 15:2, and four times in Ps 18, including in the well-known v. 25 "with the blameless you show yourself blameless". Pss 15, 18, and 19 (and on to 24) have been shown to be part of a chiastic set with Ps 19 in the center.[29]

V. 2 has lower rankings than v. 1 in all eight categories in Tables 2–5. This drop in both symbolic lemmas and factors sets off the first verse as more prominent. The greatest difference is with alphabetic factor counts. In Table 2, v. 1 is 7th with 118.18%, and v. 2 is 21st with 72.73%. In Table 5 with cola totals, v. 1 is 6th with 115.38%, and v. 2 is 20th with only 69.23%. All 8 of the alphabetical symbolic lemmas in v. 2 are theological. The low rankings resemble vv. 12–14A with rankings lower than the final secondary peak v. 14B. As noted above, I propose that the function of these low symbolic-number lines is to set off the greater numerical symbolism in the first and last lines of Ps 19. The repetition of "day to day" and "night to night" begins a serial repetition that builds up to the peak in 6B. The repeated preposition *l*=30 has the YHW(H) factors of 10, 6, and 5. The first colon has divine-name factors of 32 and 17, and the second has the repeated *lylh* 'night' =39 or 13x3. Also, note that 39 is 26+13, relating to *YHWH*=26. The last lemma

---

28. Note Craigie (*Psalms 1–50*, 182) concerning "God" in the first poem 1–6, and "*YHWH*" in the second poem 7–9, "The glories of nature indicate God (אֵל v 2) in general terms, whereas the glories of the *Torah* reveal the Lord (יהוה, vv 8–10)".

29. Brown ("Here Comes the Sun" 260).

in v. 2 is *dʕt* 'knowledge' =42 (6x7), with 6=W as one of the letters of *YHWH*, and where 7 brings the idea of fullness, especially in association with the Wisdom emphasis on "knowledge." Note that in the Wisdom book Proverbs *dʕt* 'knowledge' comes 40 times, which is another number of fullness. The first is Pro 1:7a "The fear of the Lord is the beginning of knowledge" with the same subject as Ps 19:9 "The fear of the Lord is pure, enduring forever."

V. 3—There is a clear difference in v. 3 between the high rankings in the two alphabetical Tables 2 and 5 and the low rankings in mathematical Tables 3 and 4. Table 2 has 4th place for both lemmas and factors, and Table 5 has 6th for lemmas and 9th for factors. However, Table 3 has v. 3 the 20th for lemmas and factors, and Table 4 has 19th for both. The mathematical counts thereby continue the drop in symbolic lemmas noted above after v. 1, while the higher alphabetical counts give v. 3 symbolic number prominence.

Verse 3 is the first of the two adjacent lines with 26 letters, giving them theological prominence. The first colon has 100% of its five alphabetical lemmas with theological numbers, and the second colon has two of its three lemmas theological. This gives 87.5% of the lemmas with theological values, which is the 4th highest of the 22 lines. *Dbr* 'word' has the highest divine-name value of 26 and comes 22 times in Ps 119. The lemma *ʔmr* 'speech' =34 or twice the divine-name number 17. The two *ʔyn* 'no, nor' =25 with factors 5x5 in the first colon match the *šmʕ* 'hear' =50 with alphabetical factors 10x5, making numerical parallelism with the second colon. The mathematical count 410 has factors 10x41 and 5x82, bringing the total of the factor 5 to five times. Six comes in two lemmas with *w* 'and' having the alphabetical factor =6 and mathematical [6], and *bly*=24 (6x4) and [42=7x6], totaling four times. The letters of *YHWH* are well represented by factors of 10, 6, and 5. The high number of theological numbers complements the 26-letter line, giving v. 3 strong numerical prominence. Zinner notes that besides v. 3 being a 26-letter line, there are 26 words beginning with the superscription (Hebrew v. 1) and ending with v. 3.[30]

---

30. Zinner ("Psalm 19," 2019, 27).

POSITION IN THE CLINES AND NUMERIC EMBELLISHMENT

V. 4A—In Tables 2–5, 4A is low in the ranking for lemmas, having alphabetical counts of 10th, 12th, and mathematical 16th and 19th. The rankings for factors vary with high counts for alphabetical counts at 8th and 10th place, but low for mathematical at 21st and 17th in Tables 3 and 4. 4A is the second 26-letter line in Ps 19 and follows immediately after the other one in v. 3. The fact that these two 26-letter lines come together strengthens the semantic connection between the two lines of the stanza. Alphabetical counts with YHWH numbers strengthen numeric cohesion for three synonyms—*ʔmr* 'speech' =34 (**17**x2) in 3a, *dbr* 'words' =**26** in 3a, and *mlh* 'words' =30 (**10**x3, **5**x**6** the three letters in YHWH) in 4Ab. The numerical pattern has both the short and full divine-name numbers 17 and 26 in the first colon of v. 3 and their synonym with factors of 10, 5, and 6 in the last colon of the stanza in 4Ab. The numbers 5 and 6 are reinforced with *qw* 'line' =25 (5x5) in 4Aa and *tbl* 'world' =36 (6x6) in 4Ab, which are both symbolically strong because of the double 5 and 6. Another divine-name number comes in 4Aa with *kl* 'all' =23 based on values of *kbwd* 'glory'. The number 39, which comes in 4Aa with *ʔrṣ* 'earth' =39, is also a special theological number relating to the 26 of YHWH because it is the sum of 26 and its prime number base 13. Mathematical counts in 4A are similarly high with 11 symbolic counts, including two 10 and 5 combinations recalling YH, and a 23, three more 5's, and two 6's. There is also another 39 with its 26+13 with *qšh*=195 having factors 13x15, and 5x39. The factor 5 is predictable in any lemma with only letters ending with zero and an *h*=5. The plethora of these theological lemmas in these two 26-letter lines, 3 and 4A, strengthens the evidence of numerical embellishment as a tool in biblical Hebrew.

V. 4B is the beginning of the second stanza of the first poem, and semantically connects to the following v. 5. It is a short trimeter monocolon line and considered a secondary peak. All eight rankings for symbolic numbers in Tables 2–5 are higher than average in the clines for 4B—one is ranked 2nd (with a mathematical 220% in Table 3); one is marked 3rd (with 200 in Table 4); the two in Table 5 are ranked 4th; others are one 6th, two 9th, and one 10th.

Verse 4B is the only line in Ps 19 with 200+ in two tables, which shows a special significance, probably related to its introducing "sun". "Sun" has very strong divine-name factors, including a 32 by mathematical counts where *šmš*=640 32x20, 10x64, and 5x128, and by alphabetical factors is 55 (11x5), which can relate to the double 5=*h* in YHWH. The preceding clitic lemma *l* 'for' =12 has an alphabetical factor of 6 and mathematical factors of 10, 6, and 5 representing the letters in YHWH. "Set" (*śm*) =34 has a factor of 17, the short count for YHWH, and has alliteration with the previous word *šmš* 'sun'. *ʔhl* 'tent' =18 (6x3) [36 6x6] has three factors of six, and sometimes refers to God's dwelling place, the Tabernacle (1Ch 17:5; Ps 15:1). This plethora of divine-name factors in the line introducing the "sun" adds support for an analogous relationship between "sun" and YHWH in Ps 19.

The alphabetical factor 11 in "sun" (55=11x5) is the prime number base of the alphabetic 22-set, which is important in marking junctures. The alphabetical total of the lemma values in 4B is 121 or 11x11. Having these three 11s in 4B could be a pointer to the structural juncture of starting a new stanza. (Also note the 22 and 44 marking the closure in the last v. 14 of Ps 19.) All lemmas and cola totals except *b*=2 are symbolic for both alphabetical and mathematical counts. The high counts in 4B in this first line of a stanza resemble the high counts in 1a, the first of the whole psalm, and in vv. 7–8A that begin the Torah poem. They all show a greater presence of symbolic lemmas in opening lines.

V. 5 is ranked in the lower half of all but three of the eight clines in Tables 2–5, ranging from 13th to 20th. The exceptions are with alphabetical factors in Tables 2 and 5, with the 9th, 10th, and 11th. The ratio of symbolic lemmas to total lemmas in Table 5 is a low 60%. Of the 8 alphabetical symbolic lemmas, only 4 are from the theological set {*w*=6, *hwʔ*=12 (6x2), *ḥph*=30 (10x3, 5x6), and *l*=12 (6x2)}, and four are from the 22-alphabetic set (*k*=11 comes twice, *ḥtn*=44 (11x4), and *rwṣ*=44 (11x4). These from the 22-set are structured beautifully, combining the base 11 of the set, and 44, the doublet of 22. Both 11 and 44 come once in each colon. This looks like parallelism by numbers since *ḥtn* 'bridegroom' and

POSITION IN THE CLINES AND NUMERIC EMBELLISHMENT

rwṣ 'run' are the only two lemmas in the first poem that have the value 44, and they come in parallel cola. They are preceded by the lemma *k* 'as/like' =11, which adds to the prominence of the 22-set. Mathematical symbolic numbers come with eight lemmas—*k*=20 (10x2, and 5x4) twice, *mn*=90 (10x9, 6x15m 5x18), *śwś*=606 (6x101), *l*=30 (10x3, 6x5), and *ʔrḥ* 209 (11x9) besides *w*=6, and *hwʔ*=12 (6x2) which are the same as alphabetical counts since they are made up of only the first nine letters. These eight lemmas have *YHWH* counts 10, 6, and 5 twice, and YH counts twice giving divine-name numerical prominence to v. 5. The mathematical colon total 780 for 5a is highly symbolic with factors 26x30, 13x60, 10x78, 6x130, and 5x156, with 26 and 10, 6, and 5 pointing to *YHWH*. The full emphatic pronoun *hwʔ* 'it/he' referring to the "sun" in 5A can be either neuter or masculine—a thing or a person. This ambiguity may be a further clue for including "God" as a hidden analogous referent along with "sun" for the subject of 5–6. Since pronominal affixes on verbs carry agreement, independent subject pronouns are optional and are used for emphasis, which would also be expected in a divine analogy. This is also facilitated since *šmš* 'sun' in 4B can be either feminine or masculine, and the masculine is used here to apply to "bridegroom" and possibly to God by analogy.[31]

V. **6A** is the next to the last line in the first poem. The eight rankings in Tables 2–5 for symbolism are mainly low, with five in the lower halves varying between 13th and 16th. The remaining three are near the bottom of the upper halves, with 9th, 10th, and 11th. These low rankings set off the higher rankings in the following final peak 6B. An ABBA reversal comes in 6A with the first colon beginning with a prepositional phrase "From the end of the heavens" followed by the subject "(is) its-going-forth". In contrast, 6Ab begins with the subject "and-its-circuit" followed by another prepositional phrase "to their ends". This inverted parallelism makes an inclusio with *qṣh* 'end' coming in the first and last words. *Qṣh* has the value of 42, and another lemma *mwṣh*

---

31. BDB, 1139, notes "sun" as feminine in Jos 19:14, and masculine in Gen 19:23.

'going forth' at the end of 6Aa also has the value of 42. As noted above, the threefold repetition of 42 has numerical prominence. The factors of 42 are 6 and 7, and 7 means completion. This adds to the symbolism of the inclusio of *qṣh* 'end' marking v. 6 as the "end" of the first poem.

V. 6B is the final peak of the first poem in Ps 19:1–6. It is a trimeter with 13 letters, which is prominent both because of its trimeter shortness and because 13 is half of 26 and the prime number base of the multiples in the 26 set. In Table 4 it is 1st for factors with a ratio of 13/6=216.67%, and in Table 3 it is tied for 2nd at 220%. Alphabetical factors for 6B are 4th in Table 5. These high rankings show the large number of symbolic factors that mark this final peak of the first poem. As a final line, it is also consistent with high rankings at junctures throughout Ps 19, as shown in the following vv. 7–8A. The last lemma is *ḥmh* 'heat' with the value of 26. This most important divine-name number makes a numerically powerful closure to the poem. The first two lemmas, *w* 'and' and *ʾyn* 'not', have the alphabetical factors of 6 and 5x5, which are the values of W and H in *YHWH*. The mathematical counts are strong with *str* 'hide' 660=22x30, 11x60, 10x66, 6x110, 5x132, and *mn* 'from' 90=10x9, 6x15, 5x18, both with 10, 6, and 5 for YHW(H). "Hide" also has 22 and 11, which are often used to create poetic structural beauty. Colon totals also add to the theological symbolism with alphabetical 115 (5x23) with a divine-name number 23 and a 5, and mathematical 940 (10x94, 5x188) with a 10 and 5 as in YH.

The final 6B is a trimeter which can be analyzed as a discontinuous bicolon going together with the trimeter 4Ba "In them he has set a tent for the sun" as the second colon "And there is nothing hidden from its heat." 4Ba is the introductory line for the last stanza, and 6B is the final line of the first poem in Ps 19, making an inclusio of trimeters for the stanza. The impossibility of hiding from the sun's heat suggests applying it as an analogy for God's inescapable divine knowledge and reaction to both good and bad human actions and thoughts. Note the end of the second poem in vv. 11–14 with its focus on "errors," "hidden faults," and "sins."[32]

V. 7A is the first line of the second poem, and its ranking comes 1st with 100% in Tables 3 and 4 for lemmas. It also comes 2nd for mathematical factors in Table 3 with 220%, and 2nd in Table 4, which includes cola totals, with 214%. However, for Tables 2 and 5, alphabetical lemmas come last, and factors are 18th and 21st. The reason is a unique numerical enhancement that isolates two words—*YHWH* 'Lord' and *npš* 'soul'—in "The law of the Lord is perfect, reviving the soul." The only symbolic word in the alphabetical system of counting for the first colon 7Aa is the divine name *YHWH*=26. Similarly, 7Ab has only one alphabetical symbolic lemma with *npš* 'soul,' which has the value of 52 and factors of 26x2, giving a double 26 relating to the single 26 of *YHWH* in 7Aa. All other lemmas in 7A are not alphabetically symbolic, giving it a low ratio of 40%. This is an unusual but effective way to focus on YHWH—by excluding other alphabetical symbolic lemmas in the first line of this poem. Another way *YHWH* is put in focus is that there are 26 words starting with the first *YHWH* in v. 7A and ending with the sixth in v. 9B that ends the series, setting off this repetition numerically.[33] *YHWH* is the second word in all six bicolon lines in vv. 7–9, making the parallelism strong between all of them.

In contrast to 7A, in 7B every lemma is symbolic, making it 1st with the highest ratios of 100% for lemmas in Tables 2 and 3, and 1st with 240% for mathematical factors in Table 3. This is further enhanced in that the sum of all mathematical lemma values for v. 7A+B has the highest total of any of the verse counts in the poem with 3,120, and the high number of five theological factors—**26**x120, **13**x240, **10**x312, **6**x520, and **5**x624—factors that include the main theological count of *YHWH*=26 and the values of its three different consonants Y=10, W=6, and H=5. (Five factors also come with two lemmas—"heavens," the first

---

32. Goldengay, *Psalms*, 283, relates vv. 6 and 12 that have a common סתר 'hide'.

33. See Zinner "Psalm 19," 27.

word of Ps 19, and "hidden," which comes in the peak at 6B and in 12b.) The pattern in 7A of limiting the alphabetical symbolic lemmas to one with divine-name numbers in each colon contrasts with the very high counts in the rest of the verse and sets 7A off in a unique and beautiful way.

Twrh 'Torah/teaching' and *tmym* 'perfect' are both in the first verse of Pss 19 and 119, showing their close relationship. Ps 119:1 reads, "Happy are those whose way is blameless (*tmym*), who walk in the law of the Lord." *Twrh*, which is prominent in Ps 19 as the first word of its second poem, comes 25 times in Ps 119 as the primary keyword.[34] The factor 7x70 is appropriately strong with *tmym* 'perfect, complete, whole, entire' since it shares the same semantic field as "fullness" for 7. Its value of 490 also has factors 10x49 and 5x98, with 10 and 5 the values of YH. The factor 49 is 7x7, 98 is 7x14, and 70 is 7x10, further emphasizing the number 7 in each of the three non-symbolic factors. This would make the lemma *tmym* likely to be well-known and therefore to be available to give emphasis as in the first lines of Pss 19 and 119. Note that *tmym* comes four times in Ps 18, and twice in Ps 119, which are both associated with Ps 19.

V. **7B** has high counts, giving it 1st place in three places in Tables 2 and 3 as noted above. In Table 5 it is in 2nd place for both lemmas and factors, and in Table 4 in 3rd place. 7Ba is especially high with mathematical symbolic factors 8/3=266.67%. The first lemma *ʿdwt* 'decrees' is highly symbolic with alphabetical counts of 48 (6x8) and mathematical [480 32x15, 10x48, 6x80, 5x96] with the divine-name number 32 and the 10, 6, and 5 of YHW(H). *ʿdwt* comes 23 times in Ps 119, the same as *mšpṭ* 'ordinances,' which comes in Ps 19:9Ba. It comes together with *ʾmn* in Ps 93:5, as here in Ps 19:7B. In Ps 119:88, *ʿdwt pyk* 'decrees of your mouth' is highly marked by coming as the central two words

---

34. Freedman, (*Psalm 119: The Exaltation of Torah*, 33) notes that the 25 *twrh* is a larger number than any other content word in Ps 119. YHWH comes 24 times, including "law of YHWH" in the first verse, which is the only place the two come together in a construct chain.

of Ps 119.³⁵ Furthermore, the term *ʕdwt* is used for the two stone tablets of the "decrees," "testimony," or "covenant" in Exodus, Leviticus, Numbers, and Joshua, especially with "ark of *ʕdwt*" and "tabernacle of *ʕdwt*." In coronation ceremonies (2 Kg: 11:12), and in Deuteronomy, and many Psalms it is equivalent to Torah, with reference to the root meaning of "witness" and "warn."³⁶

The first word in the second colon 7Bb is *ḥkm* 'make wise'. It has the alphabetical value of 32, the *kbwd* 'glory' divine-name number, which is also found as a mathematical factor in 7Ba with *ʕdwt*. The two 32s give beautiful numerical parallelism to the two cola. "Make wise" is followed by *pty* 'simple' with the value of 490 mathematically. It has numerical parallelism with *tmym* 'perfect' in 7Aa, also with 490 and its factors of 10x49, 5x98, and 7x70. The 10s and 5s connect to the divine name YH, and the 7x70s emphasizes completeness and perfection in this first verse of the Torah poem. The first colon 7Ba also has a factor of 7 with alphabetical *ʔmn*=28 (7x4). *Pty* 'simple' and *ḥkm* 'wise' are a Wisdom word-pair (see Prov 21:11), giving them prominence.³⁷

The alphabetical total of the four lemma values in 7Ba is 102, with factors of 17x6, with 17 the short count for *YHWH*, and 6=W. The mathematical total of the whole line 7B is 1155, with factors of 5, 11, and 7, one of each of the three sets of symbolic numbers, and adding another 7.

---

35. Yoder and Zinner (*Psalm 119*, 32) write of *ʕdwt*, "The lynchpin role of v. 88's noun עדות is congruent with the fact that in a non-emended MT Ps 119 text of a total of 1064 words, this noun is the absolute mathematical center, the psalm's 532nd word (532x2=1064)." Also note that 532 has the factors of 7x76, with "fullness" symbolized by 7, which comes twice counting from each end to *ʕdwt pyk* in the center. The values of *pyk* are also significant. The lemma *py* has the mathematical value of 90=10x9 and 5x18 with the YH factors 10+5. The surface form *pyk* has the alphabetical count of 36=6x6, and the mathematical 110=55x2, both with 6s and 5s as the middle letters of YHWH.

36. "Key Terms of the Old Testament" in SIL and United Bible Societies' translation program, *Paratext*, entry 121.

37. Zinner (*Psalm 119*, 89–90) points to "The unfolding of your words gives light; it imparts understanding to the simple" in Ps 119:130 "as the inspiration behind" the "simple" in Ps 19:7[8]B.

V. 8A has a fairly high 3rd rank in all counts in the mathematical Tables 3 and 4, but lower ranks in the alphabetical Tables 2 (7th and 5th) and 5 (17th and 7th). The interesting difference is between 8A and the next line 8B. Compare the figures below, which are copied from the details of v. 8 in the "Line by Line Analysis" above.

	Alphabetical		Mathematical	
	Sym. lemmas	Sym. factors	Sym. lemmas	Sym. factors
8A	4/5=80%	6/5=120%	5/5=100%	11/5=220%
8B	3/5=60%	5/5=100%	3/5=60%	5/5=140%

As noted above, the high counts in 8A are a continuation of the high counts at the juncture of the two poems from 6B–8A. The 220% for mathematical factors in 8A identifies strong prominence and places 8A among structurally significant lines with over 200%. The mathematical factor count for its first colon 8Aa is 300% and is one of the two highest *colon* totals, along with 12b. All lemmas in 8A are symbolic for both alphabetical and mathematical counts except the first, *pqwdym* 'precepts', which is only symbolic with mathematical counts. Its factors are highly symbolic with 10, 6, and 5, the letters of YHW(H). It comes 21 times in Ps 119. The second word is *YHWH* with factors of 26 and 13 in both counting systems. *Yšr* 'right', the third lemma in 8Aa, also has 10, 6, and 5 mathematically. It also has a 17, the short count for *YHWH*, strikingly in both its alphabetical and mathematical factors. Verse 8Ab has the alphabetical factor 7 in both of its lemmas and a 6 in the first lemma. Mathematical counts have the divine-name 32 for *lb* 'heart' and a 6, and the colon total has 10 and 5 as YH. This plethora of symbolic numbers gives high prominence to 8A.

V. 8B— The sharp drop in mathematical factors from 220% in 8A to 140% in 8B accentuates the high ranks of the previous lines 6B–8A at the juncture of the two poems. The contrast starts with the first word *mṣwt* 'commandments', which comes 22 times in Ps

119 but is not symbolic alphabetically or mathematically. The three previous lines in the Torah poem have mathematically symbolic lemmas found in Ps 119 that do have theological factors as their first-word subjects—"Torah" 13, "decrees" 32, 10, 6, 5, and "precepts" 10, 6, 5. Other than *YHWH*=26, one other symbolic lemma comes in each colon. 8Ba has the alphabetical *br* 'pure' =22, and 8Bb has *ʿyn* 'eye', with its value of 39 being a frequent theological number having the value of 26+13, and 13x3. The second colon and the line totals also have symbolic factors with 8Bb having the alphabetical total of 66 or 22x3 and 11x6. And the mathematical total of 1,947 for the whole v. 8 has factors of 11x177. Ranks are low for 8B (two 20th, a 19th, two 17th, and a 12th). Only Table 2 has higher rankings with an 8th and an 11th. The dramatic drop in symbolism highlights the previous lines at the juncture of 6B–8A.

V. 9A has the highest percentage for both alphabetical symbolic lemmas and factors in both Tables 2 and 5. Lines 9A and 7B are unique in Ps 19, with 100% of the alphabetical lemmas and both cola totals being symbolic numbers. These high percentages indicate a special input of symbolic numbers for this verse. The subject "the fear of the Lord," which is exceptional since it is not in Ps 119, is highlighted by these high percentages, giving focus to it. The total of six symbolic factors makes *ṭhwr* 'pure' in 9A almost as prominent as *mtwq* "sweet" in v. 10. The mathematical counts are all symbolic, except the total of 9Ab. The three lemmas in 9Aa are unique with identical factors for both alphabetical and mathematical counts. *YHWH*, as always, has identical factors 26 and 13 for both *alphabetical and mathematical* counts since the four letters are less than 11. *Yrʔh* 'fear' has duplicated alphabetical factors 6x6 and mathematical 6x6x6. The predicate *ṭhwr* 'pure' has the YH factors 10 and 5 in both the alphabetical and mathematical counts, as well as an 11. This numerical enhancement by all three lemmas having duplicate alphabetical and mathematical factors gives very strong prominence to 9Aa. These repeats are also all theological numbers. The middle letters of *ṭhwr* are the same *hw* as the middle letters of *YHWH*, which probably also made it attractive as a choice for this seemingly unusual predicate for "fear of the Lord".

The alphabetical count total of 102 for 9Aa has both the short count of 17 for *YHWH* and another 6. The 22-set is especially strong with the mathematical total of 462 for 9Aa with factors of 77x6, 66x7, 22x21, and 11x42, having four doublets of identical digits. Besides these doublets, 220, the mathematical value of *ṭhwr* 'pure' in the first colon, has doublets of 44x5, 22x10, and 11x20. The first lemma of 9Ab *ʿmd* 'endure' also has the alphabetical value 33 with a factor of 11. The second lemma *l* with values of 12 and [30] has another alphabetical 6 and the mathematical factors 10, 6, and 5, the values of the letters of *YHW(H)*. The third lemma *ʿd* has the alphabetical factors of 10 and 5 as in YH, and adds alliteration by having two of the same letters as *ʿmd*. This plethora of multiples of 11 of the 22-alphabetic-set and varied combinations of the 26-set gives strong focus to the theme of "the fear of the Lord" in v. 9.

V. 9B comes 2nd for alphabetical factors in Table 2, and 7th in Table 5. However, mathematical counts are low, placing 9B 15th in Table 3, and 16th in Table 4. V. 9B is the last of the six Torah lines with the repeated "of the Lord." These repetitions serve as a build-up to the central peak in 10A. All lemmas except *ṣdq* are symbolic by alphabetical and mathematical counts. Mathematical counts of factors are generally low, accounting for the above 15th and 16th rankings. The first lemma *mšpṭ* 'ordinances' has the most factors with alphabetical 60 (10x6, 5x12) and mathematical 429 (13x33 and 11x39, with 39 a theological number since 39=26+13). *Mšpṭ* comes 23 times in Ps 119, the same as *ʿdwt* 'decrees' in 7Ba, and similar to *mṣwt* 'commandments' in 8Ba, which comes 22 times in Ps 119. *Mšpṭ* and *ṣdq* are a frequent word pair (see Ps 143:2). The first colon total has a mathematical factor of 32 (and a 7), and the second has the alphabetical factor of 23, adding symbolism by the two *kbwd* divine-name numbers.

V. 10A is the central peak of the second poem. It has 17 letters, the short count for *YHWH*. The alphabetical value of *pz*=26 'fine gold' is the same as the full count for *YHWH*=26, giving another embellishment to the peak line. *Pz rb* 'fine-gold much' comes at the end of 10Ab. This is especially significant since the final peak 6B of the first poem ends with another alphabetical 26-letter lemma *ḥmh* 'heat'. In 10Aa *ḥmd* 'desire' has the mathematical value of 52 or double 26, making a 26x2//26 numerical parallelism in 10A. "Desire" also has the alphabetical value 25 with two factors of 5, as in the two *H*s in *YHWH*. The first lemma in the first word is the article *h*, with the value of 5, and the first in 10Ab is *w* 'and' with the value of 6, giving cola-initial *YHWH* numbers in both alphabetical and mathematical counts. The preposition *mn* 'from', with mathematical factors 10, 6, and 5 as in YHW(H), comes in both cola, also giving divine-name numerical parallelism. *Zhb* 'gold' has the value of 14 in both alphabetical and mathematical counts since the values of its letters are all less than 11. This gives the factor 7 in both counts.

Mathematical counts for both cola totals are symbolic with 10Aa having factors of the divine-name number 23 and a 7, and 10Ab having another 7, a 5x77, and an 11. These sevens, together with the two with *zhb*, likely point to an attention to make the peak line special. The intensification of the second element, which is a recognized feature in Hebrew parallelism, is clear in 10A with "gold" followed by "much fine gold" with its value of 26.

Having *mn* in both cola lowers ratios since it is not symbolic alphabetically, and having *pz* in 10Ab lowers ratios since it is not symbolic mathematically. In Table 4, mathematical counts including colon totals have 10A in 7th place for both lemmas and factors. The lines ranked 1st–6th ahead of 10A are all structural high points, and the final secondary peak 14B is tied with 7th for lemmas, so in comparison to the rest of the lines, Table 4 puts the peak line 10A in the group showing special numerical embellishment. However, in Table 3, without cola totals, lemmas are 10th and factors are 13th. Alphabetical factor counts in Table 2 are 10th, but the other alphabetical counts in Tables 2 and 5 are low (14th, 17th, and 21st).

The peak 10A is set off by coming in the center of a metrical chiasm 555554 4 455555(3). The three 4s in the center are exceptional. Both 10A and 10B have only two words per colon, making four words per line, and the Masoretic Text in 9B has the first two words (*mšpṭy-YHWH*) in the first colon joined by a hyphen, making four stress units for it, matching 10B. Other lines in the second poem vv. 7–14A are fairly consistent with a 3-2 cola pattern making five stress units. The exceptional final trimeter is a secondary peak marked by its shortness and its special spiritual message with the seventh *YHWH*, "O Lord, my rock and my redeemer."

"Gold" comes twice in Ps 119—in v. 72 describing the words of the Torah, and in v. 127 along with "fine gold" describing "your commandments."

Although line totals are not always included, that of the peak line 10A is uniquely prominent, as noted in the "Introduction." The 10A mathematical total 546 has factors of 26x21, 13x42, 6x91, 7x78, (and also separately 546=39x14 with 39=26+13). Amazingly, six of the factors that are not symbolic have symbolic factors of their own (21, 42, and 91 are multiples of 7; 78 is a multiple of 26, 13 and 6; 39 is a multiple of 13; and 14 is another multiple of 7). All of these symbolic numbers are in the *YHWH*-set or the seven-set, none in the 22-set. The striking thing is that the same number 546 comes in the first word of the next line 10B for the mathematical value of *mtwq* 'sweet,' forming a beautiful numerical parallelism by this highly symbolic number.

V. 10B has 100% of its mathematical lemmas symbolic, tying five other lines for 1st place in Table 3. In Table 4, 10B is 2nd since the cola total for 10Bb is not mathematically symbolic. The mathematical *factor* count in Table 3 is 200%, tying with two other lines for 5th place. 10B is in 6th place in Table 4. However, alphabetical counts for lemmas are low, with 17th in Table 2 and 15th in Table 5. Alphabetical factors are 16th in Table 2 and 15th in Table 5. The high counts for mathematical lemmas are likely a result of 10B being parallel to 10A and in the same verse as this peak line. The parallelism is enhanced to be "sweeter than honey" by the first word *mtwq* 'sweet' having the *same value 546 as the total mathematical lemma counts of 10A*. As noted above, *mtwq* has the highest number of six symbolic factors, with alphabetical factors 10 and 6, and a plethora of mathematical factors—26x21,

13x42, 6x91, 7x78, and 39x14, with 39 being special as the sum of 26+13. Also, the preposition *mn* 'from', which is in each colon of 10A, now comes in 10Ba with its high mathematical factors 10, 6, and 5 as in YHW(H). *Dbš* 'honey' has a mathematical factor of 17, the short count for *YHWH*, and the alphabetical value of *npt* 'drip' is 52 or double the 26 of *YHWH*. The mathematical factors of *npt* are 10 and 5 as YH. Numerical parallelism comes with this 52 and that of *ḥmd* in 10Aa. Both cola in 10B begin with *w*, which has the value of 6 for both alphabetical and mathematical counts. The last word *ṣwp* 'honeycomb', has mathematical factors of 22 and 11. The alphabetical total of 10Bb is 99 with a factor of 11, giving numerical attention to poetic structure in this final line of the stanza.

The totals for 10Ba have alphabetical factors 10 and 5, and mathematical factors 6. The mathematical total 1660 (10x166 and 5x332) for all of 10B has the YH factors 10 and 5. The many symbolic numbers give prominence to 10B, and to the whole verse, including its previous central peak of the second poem.

V. 11 has no symbolic mathematical lemmas or factors in 11a and only one in 11b. 11a is the only colon with no mathematical symbolic lemmas, and neither of the colon totals has mathematical symbolism. It stands in the lowest 22nd rank in the mathematical Tables 3 and 4 for lemmas and factors. There is a reason for the lack of symbolism. The only mathematical symbolic lemma in 11b is *šmr* 'keeping' with the YHW(H) factors of 10, 6, and 5. This is an effective way to highlight "keeping" God's ordinances as a personal responsibility. "Keep" has a pronominal suffix -*ām* 'them' for which the antecedent is *mšpty-yhwh* 'ordinances of YHWH' in 9Ba. The same suffix with the same antecedent "ordinances" comes on the first lemma of v. 11 with "by them." "Ordinances" continues as a subject of the sentence through v. 10 comparing them to gold in the peak line and to honey in 10B, and then continues as an object in each colon of v. 11. *Mšpṭ* has a broad meaning, including "ordinances" by a ruler or by God as here, and also "judgments" in a court case, and "justice". It comes 65 (13x5) times in the Psalms.

The full colon 11B reads: "in keeping them there is great reward", giving a positive meaning following the admonition in the first colon of being "warned" by them, which is a reminder that there are negative results of not keeping them. The process of limiting symbolic lemmas to emphasize one or two lemmas with symbolism is similar to v. 7 with $YHWH=26$ and $npš=52$ as the only alphabetical symbolic lemmas in its two cola, giving numerical parallelism. The difference is that 7A, as the first line of the second poem, has mathematical lemmas that place it in 1st place in Tables 2 and 3, and 2nd place for factors in Tables 3 and 4, while v. 11 stays at the bottom of the mathematical ranks. The unique lowest rank in v. 11 also gives prominence to this first line of a stanza, which elsewhere in Ps 10 is marked by high ranks. The common denominator in these markings is the quantity of symbolism, either high or lowest. Each colon has an alphabetical 22 lemma—$ʿbd$ 'servant' and rb 'great'—giving numerical parallelism. There is distant parallelism with 9Aa having "fear of the Lord" semantically similar to zhr "warned" in 11a, the line on the other side of the peak 10Aa. The alphabetical value of zhr is 32, a divine-name number, which makes it prominent.

Alphabetical rankings for v. 11 are also low, with 21st in Table 2 for lemmas and 19th for factors, but cola totals raise alphabetical ranks to 12th for lemmas and 10th for factors in Table 5. The first colon has an alphabetical total of 72 with factors 6x12, and the second colon has 115 with factors 5x23. This 23 is interesting, especially along with 32 of zhr, since both are $kbwd$ divine-name numbers. Although it is not counted in the above tables, the alphabetical verse total of 187 has factors of 17x11 with the short count of $YHWH$, and 11 as the base of the 22-set. The overall picture for v. 11 is that rankings are low, and the noted symbolic cola and verse totals do not raise ranks sufficiently to highlight the verse. As the verse after the central peak, a low count follows the pattern seen in the drop in 8B after the high ranks in 7A–8A.

V. 12—12b is unique by having one of the two highest 300% cola and one of the two lowest 0% cola. The 300% is for mathematical factors, and the 0% is for both alphabetical lemmas and factors. The other 300% is 8Aa. The other 0% is the previous 11a, creating a special numerical parallelism.

Line rankings are generally low for v. 12, with Table 2 having the alphabetical counts 20th for lemmas and 17th for factors, and Table 5 being similar with 13th for lemmas and 17th for factors. Mathematical counts in Table 3 are 6th and 7th, and in Table 4 are 10th and 11th. The low numbers, especially the 0% cola, continue the low counts in v. 11, thereby setting off the prior peak in v. 10. Low counts continue to the final secondary peak in v. 14B, making it more prominent with its higher counts.

In contrast to 12b, 12a has all three alphabetical lemmas symbolic with *byn* 'detect' having the YHWH value of 26, *my* 'who' the divine name 23, and *šgyʔh* 'errors' =40 with the factors 10 and 5 of YH. These are all strong theological numbers. The strongest, *byn*=26 'understand, detect, discern', is a Wisdom word coming ten times in Ps 119. Mathematical counts have symbolic factors of 10 and 5 and an 11 in 12a, and in 12b a 10, 6, and 5 for both *mn* 'from' and *str* 'hidden'. "Hidden" also has a 22 and 11, and *nqh* 'clear' has a 5. The only symbolic colon total in v. 12 is 12b, which has a mathematical factor of 5. *Str* 'hidden' =660 22x30, 11x60, 10x66, 6x110, 5x132 mathematically, is highly symbolic, having one of the two lemmas with five symbolic factors. The other is *šmym* 'heavens' in 1Aa and 6Aa. "Hidden" is repeated from the peak in 6B, where nothing is "hidden" from the sun. Similarly, what is "hidden" in 12b is not hidden from God, who can "clear ... hidden faults." The change from self-examination with "warned" in 11a, to a prayer "clear me from hidden faults" in 12b, begins personal "me/I" statements that continue to the end of the psalm.

Two Wisdom texts with similar Wisdom words as these in Ps 19:12—one from Ps 107:43, and one from Hosea 14:9[10]—are discussed next along with their symbolic numbers. The comparison of the three is remarkable.

The last v. 43 of Ps 107 has the advice "Whoever is wise let him consider" similar to Ps 19:12, with the Wisdom word *byn* 'understand, consider' =26, and *my* 'who' =23. Ps 107 also has the other half of a common word pair *ḥkm* 'be wise', which comes in

Ps 19:7B. It also has *šmr* 'give heed' translated "keep" in Ps 19:11. Every lemma except for *ḥsd*=27 is alphabetically symbolic (mathematically *ḥsd*=72 or **6**x**12**). The NRSV and Hebrew texts, and their alphabetical count analysis of Ps 107:43 follow: "Let those who are wise give heed to these things, and consider the steadfast love of the Lord."

מי־חכם וישמר־אלה ויתבוננו חסדי יהוה:

my=**23**, *ḥkm*=**32**, *w*=**6**, *šmr*=54 (**6**x9), *ʔlh*=18 (**6**x3); *w*=**6**, *byn*=**26**, *ḥsd*=27, *YHWH*=**26**. The symbolic ratio is 8/9 lemmas =88.89%. Also, note that all these symbolic numbers are in the theological set.

A comparison of Ps 19:12 to Hos 14:9[10]A, which is the first line of the Wisdom poem ending the book of Hosea, also shows remarkable numerological similarities.[38] Both have the same *my*=23, and *byn*=26. Hos 14:9[10] reads in RSV: "Whoever is wise, let him understand these things; whoever is discerning, let him know them;" (מי חכם ויבן אלה נבון וידעם) or transliterated: *my ḥkm wybn ʔlh nbwn wydʕm*). This first line has eight lemmas, *all of which are symbolic* by the alphabetical count. The first two lemmas, *my* 'whoever'=23 and *ḥkm* 'wise' =32, are divine-name numbers equivalent to *kbwd* 'glory' with its alphabetical count 23, and its mathematical count of 32. This is the same as in Ps 107:43. After a *w* 'and' = 6, comes *byn*=26. This brings three of the four divine-name numbers closely together: 23, 32, and 26. The other divine-name number, 17, comes twice in the second colon copied below, with *yšr* and *ṣdq* as factors of 51 (17x3). The Wisdom word *byn*=26 'understand, detect, discern' also significantly comes a second time at the beginning of the second colon. The whole verse Hos 14:9[10] is as follows in RSV, Hebrew, and lemmas with alphabetical counts: "Whoever is wise, let him understand these things; whoever is discerning, let him know them; for the ways of the Lord are right, and the upright walk in them, but transgressors stumble in them."

---

38. For a numerical and structural discussion of Hos 14:9[10] see Bliese (*Hosea*, 210–12).

סי חכם ויבן אלה נבון וידעם כי־ישרים דרכי יהוה
וצדקים ילכו בם ופשעים יכשלו בם:

my=**23**, $ḥkm$=**32**, w=**6**, byn=**26**, $ʔlh$=18 (**6**x3); byn=**26**, w=**6**, $ydʕ$=30 (**10**x3, **5**x**6**); // ky=21 (7x3), $yšr$=51 (**17**x3), drk=35 (5x7), $YHWH$=**26**, w=**6**, $ṣdq$=51 (**17**x3), hlk=28 (7x4), b=2, w=**6**, $pšʕ$=54 (**6**x9), $kšl$=44 (**11**x4), and b=2.

The first line is 100% symbolic alphabetically, and every lemma in the second line, except the two occurrences of b=2, has symbolic factors. The ratio of 18 symbolic lemmas divided by 20 total lemmas is 90%.

For comparison with a similar but non-Wisdom verse from the main body of Hosea note 5:6. "With their flocks and herds they shall go to seek the Lord, but they will not find him; he has withdrawn from them."

בצאנם ובבקרם ילכו לבקש את־יהוה ולא ימצאו חלץ מהם:

b=2, $ṣʔn$=33 (**11**x3), w=**6**, b=2, bqr=41, hlk=28 (7x4), l=12 (**6**x2), $bqš$=42 (**6**x7), $ʔt$=**23**, $YHWH$=**26**, w=**6**, $lʔ$=**13**, $mṣʔ$=**32**, $ḥlṣ$=38, mn=27.

The ten symbolic lemmas divided by 15 total lemmas =66.67%, which contrasts with 90% in the Wisdom lines in Hos 14:9[10]A and 88.89% in Ps 107:43. The 3/6 or 50% ratio of symbolic lemmas in the first clause of Hos 5:6 "With their flocks and herds they shall go" also has a significant contrast with the 100% for the eight theological lemmas in the first line of Hos 14:9[10]Aa, the 100% for the five theological lemmas in the first colon of Ps 107:43, and the 100% for the three theological lemmas in the first colon of Ps 19:12a.

V. 13A has very low symbolic rankings—16th for lemmas and 21st for factors in alphabetical Table 2, 21st for lemmas and 19th for factors in mathematical Table 3, 21st for both lemmas and factors in mathematical Table 4 with cola totals, 18th for lemmas in alphabetical Table 5, and the lowest possible 22nd for factors with cola totals in Table 5. V. 13A is lower than 14B in all tables for both lemmas and factors. This continues low counts in vv. 11-12 leading up to the higher counts in the final secondary peak 14B.

The last colon of v. 12 begins with *mn* 'from' (hidden faults), and the first colon of v. 13 begins with *gm mn* 'also from' (presumptuous sins). *Nqh* 'clear, empty', first requesting and then expecting forgiveness from sin, comes in the second colon of both lines. This gives them double anadiplosis at the strophe juncture. *Mn* has mathematical factors of 10, 5, and 6 as YHW(H). The lemma *ḥśk*=40 'keep back' has alphabetical 10 and 5 as YH, and is parallel to the 40 of "presumptuous sins" in v. 12. Other theological counts in 13A are *mšl* with an alphabetical factor of the divine-name number 23, alphabetical *ʔl* 'not' =13 or half of 26, and the colon total for 13Ab with another 13. The theological numbers give prominence to the personal theological message.

There are also symbolic lemmas from the 22-set. *Zd* 'presumptuous sins' has the value of 11 for both alphabetical and mathematical counts, and *ʕbd* 'servant', which follows *zd*, has the alphabetical value of 22, continuing a series moving toward the end of the poem.

V. 13B has mainly low counts. Alphabetical factors are 22nd in Table 2 and 18th in Table 5. Lemmas are 19th in Table 2 and 16th in Table 5. Mathematical rankings in Tables 3 and 4 are higher with lemmas 12th and 9th, and both factor counts are 8th. This follows the pattern of the previous verses for low symbolic ratios leading up to the final secondary peak 14B with higher ratios. The only exceptions are in Tables 3 and 4, with the two mathematical factors being higher for 13B. The other six rankings have 13B lower than 14B.

Three high mathematical counts in 13B result from lemmas with consonants from only the 13 letters with final zeros. *Tmm* 'blameless' =480 with factors of the divine-name number 32, and of 10, 6, and 5, the letters of YHW(H). It also has an alphabetical factor of 6. *Mn* comes a third time after 12b and 13Aa with its 10, 6, and 5. *Pšʕ* 'transgression' =450 is a third lemma with 10, 6, and 5. It also has an alphabetical 6. *Nqh* 'innocent' =155 (5x31) has two letters from the 13 letters with zeros plus an *h*=5, a mathematical combination that always has a symbolic factor of 5.

A *w* 'and' in 13Ba has both alphabetical and mathematical 6. The lemma *rb* 'great' has the value of 22, continuing the series of the 22 set after *ʿbd*=22 in 13A. The mathematical colon total for 13Ba also has a factor of 11. The final mathematical colon total for 13B has a factor of 13, and the alphabetical total is 100 with factors 10x10 and 5x20. The even 100 in this antepenultimate line may relate to the 999 total in the penultimate 14A just before the final secondary peak 14B. The three *mn* 'from' and their objects form a buildup of progressively serious sins—"errors," "hidden faults," and "the great transgression"—tying vv. 12 and 13 together. I propose that the similarities between vv. 12 and 13 were designed to complement each other by their low counts, similar numerology, and similar themes.

V. 14A continues the low symbolic number counts of vv. 11–13. Table 4 ranks lemmas 17th and factors 13th. Table 3 has them 13th and 12th. Table 5 has 8th and 13th, and Table 2 has 5th and 9th. Only three of the eight rankings in the four tables are higher for 14A than for 14B— alphabetical lemmas in Table 2, and mathematical factors in Tables 3 and 4.

Although most ratios are low, there is a high total of 24 symbolic factors (21 theological) in 14A. The mathematical value of *hyh*=20 with YH factors of 10 and 5 comes in the first word, and *l*=30 with the YHW(H) factors of 10, 6, and 5 comes in both 14Aa and b. The alphabetical count for *ʾmr* 'words' is 34 with the divine-name factor of 17. *Ph* 'mouth' =85 mathematically has factors 17x5 and the alphabetical value of 22, continuing the 22 buildup to 14B.

In 14Ab the conjunction *w*=6 comes in both alphabetical and mathematical counts, and *lb* 'heart' has 14 alphabetically with a factor of 7, and a divine-name 32 mathematically. The last lemma *pnh* 'before' is alphabetically 36 or 6x6, and mathematically 135 with a factor of 5 (*p*=80 and *n*=50 are among the 13 letters that end in zero, plus an *h*=5. The previous *ph* in 14Aa has 85 by the same rule).

The cola totals for 14A are 722 and 277, which total 999. This is not a symbolic number by factors, but forms an interesting play on numbers between 722 and 277 with a reversal of the pattern of 7s and 2s, forming the numerically symbolic sum 999. This is ingenious and is a powerful marker for the penultimate line.

V. 14B is the final line of Ps 19 "O Lord, my rock and my redeemer." It is counted as a secondary peak since it is a monocolon. In Table 3, the mathematical cline has 14B in 1st place along with four other lines that are 100% symbolic for lemmas. This shows the numerical enhancement in this final line. Tables 4 and 5 with colon totals have it in 7th and 5th places, and in Table 2 it is 10th, which are all above average. For *factors*, in Table 5 it is 3rd, and in Table 2 it is 5th. The penultimate line 14A is less symbolic with its highest positions as 6th and 8th, and the other six positions for 14A varying from 13th to 17th. 13A and B have even lower counts. These lines with low counts before the higher final 14B set off the final secondary peak.

A special numeric buildup of alphabetic lemma values in vv. 13–14 also gives prominence to the final peak colon. The buildup begins in 13A with a lemma with the value 11, followed by a 22. Then beautifully, 13B has a second 22, and 14A has a third 22. Finally, the series ends with the 22nd line 14B with the 44-value lemma ṣwr 'rock' with factors 22x2. This is important since "rock" is the only material metaphor in Ps 19 used to describe YHWH, coming in "O Lord, my rock". *YHWH* comes here for the final 7th time and is the only place where YHWH is addressed by name.

The final lemma is *gʔl* 'redeemer' with a mathematical value of 34 and factors 17x2. This makes the first word of 14B *YHWH* begin the line with its 26, and makes "redeemer" close the line and the whole psalm with 17, the short count of *YHWH*. The alphabetical colon total is 92 with factors 23x4, giving another divine-name number 23 for 14B. A *w* 'and' comes before "redeemer" with both alphabetical and mathematical values of 6. Both "rock" and "redeemer" have the suffix "my," continuing the first-person singular close relationship of the prayer, beginning with v. 12b.

The combination of the metaphors "rock" and "redeemer" is also found in Ps 78:35, adding prominence to readers who know both psalms.[39] Craigie beautifully describes the significance of it and "rock" in the psalm, "The final words, describing the psalmist's relationship to God, transform God's universal and cosmic glory, with which the psalm began, into the glory of an intimate relationship between a human being and God, who offers solidarity and redemption."[40]

How Would an Author Create Such Numerical Embellishments?

What methods would an author use to create such number patterns? The first requirement is to add the values of the letters of lemmas to know their value. Presumably, some lemmas were well-known within literary circles as having special symbolic value and were available from memory without counting for a practiced author. The author could then find ways to use these words within a text in places where he wanted to give emphasis. Both the alphabetical-ordinal and mathematical-standard systems of calculation were available, so words could be doubly symbolic, singly symbolic, or not symbolic. Alphabetical letter counts are limited to the 1–22 values, while mathematical go up to 400 by decimals and hundreds. The larger mathematical numbers make them more difficult to calculate than alphabetical values.[41] However, this study gives evidence that both systems were used throughout Ps 19.

---

39. Zinner (*Psalm 119*, 85) notes that "rock" can be seen as "influence" from Ps 18:2[3], "redeemer" is not in Ps 18 and "can be explained by the influence of Ps 119:154".

40. Craigie (*Psalms 1–50*, 183).

41. Zinner ("Psalm 19," 2019, 26) notes the practical reason for the use of alphabetical or ordinal counts since they are not so large, "The praxis of using two different systems of gematria, standard and ordinal, in one psalm is likely based on a quite utilitarian consideration, namely, that for words in which *resh*, *shin*, and/or *tav* proliferate, it is much easier to use ordinal gematria in such cases for word/letter placements."

Another method for numerical enhancement is to adjust the number of words, lemmas, or letters in a text or portion of it. This is well documented in biblical studies, especially for keywords and for the number of words or letters in a text or special line of poetry. It would require authors to add up in a draft what they want to emphasize, and then find ways to add or subtract items to make the total symbolic. Evidence shows this is applied to either lemma or factor counts. In some cases, the number(s) would likely be chosen when some total came close to something that could be manipulated to make it symbolic. A possible example is the colon totals for 4B with alphabetical 121 having a doublet of symbolic factors 11x11, besides the mathematical 1058 with factors of 23x46 or 23x(23+23) with a triplet of divine-name 23s, to enhance the line that introduces the "sun" as analogous to God. Another possible example is the two lines of v. 14A with 277 and 722 mathematical lemma totals adding up to 999 in the last verse of the psalm, which looks more likely to be manmade rather than chance. In other cases, patterns could be formed by excluding symbolic words to emphasize an adjacent significant line more. A possible example is in the lines before the final v. 14B. Such reduction also applies to having only one special word symbolic as with *šmr* 'keeping' in the mathematical lemma counts in v. 11. The rounding of total numbers to make something symbolic would require counting all the lemmas or factors in a text or the portion in focus.

The Relationship of Psalm 19 to Psalm 119 with Reference to "Fear of the Lord"

The question, "Which came first, Ps 19 or 119?" is important to consider in regard to the many similarities between the two. Craigie notes that several scholars "have taken the wisdom character of the psalm to be indicative of an exilic or postexilic date."[42] He adds, "The second part of the psalm begins with a reflection on the law

---

42. Craigie (*Psalms 1–50*, 180). Also note p. 179 where he notes that *yrʔh* "is a good *wisdom* term in keeping with the character of the second half of the psalm.

or Torah (v 8a) of the Lord, written in a wisdom style reminiscent of Ps 119."[43] Zinner writes, "That Pss 19 and 119 are cognate texts in some way is uncontested."[44] After discussing the evidence, he concludes, "Consequently, a good case can be made that although both Pss 19 and 119 are late, Ps 19 is the later of the two."[45] Numerological data supports this. There are 176 lemmas in the poetry in Ps 19:1–14 [Hebrew 2–15] after the introduction. 176 is the same as the number of verses in Ps 119. 176 has the factors 22x8, and Ps 119 is divided into 22 strophes of 8 verses each, following the 22 letters of the alphabet. The number 176 could likely result from the author of Ps 19 constructing this total to show the relationship of Ps 19 to the well-known structure of Ps 119. However, if Ps 19 is first, a lemma total of its poetic verses would not be significant or noticeable enough to inspire the 22x8 pattern in Ps 119.

An obvious example of borrowing between Ps 19 and Ps 119 is in the list of keywords for the Torah in the first stanza of Ps 119:1–7. Zinner notes that the same words come in Ps 19:7–9 [8–10] in the same order as in Ps 119, except that *ḥq* 'decrees' in Ps 119:5 is replaced by *yrʔh* 'fear' in Ps 19:9[10][46] The result is that of

---

43. Craigie (*Psalms 1–50*, 181).

44. Zinner ("Psalm 19," 41). The number 19 in both psalms has raised another suggestion. Lenzi ("Metonic Cycle," 449) explores "the idea that the scribe responsible for the final redaction of the MT Psalter knew about the Metonic Cycle, a 19 year calendrical system that synchronized the lunar and solar years via regular intercalation, attributed a symbolic significance to the number 19 related to this number's role in creating cosmological harmony in that system, and then used 19 as a symbolic number to inform the placement of Psalms 19 and 119 in the final redaction of the MT Psalter."

45. Zinner ("Psalm 19," 2019, 42–8) discusses evidence for considering Psalm 19 to be later than Psalm 119. Before the conclusion quoted above, Zinner notes on p. 48 "what tips the balance in favor of Ps 119's chronological priority is Ps 19's use of poetic devices involving meter most closely paralleled in post-biblical Hebrew poetry." Zinner expands his argument in a draft book (*Psalm 119*, 78, 79, 81) in 2020, in which he presents both sides in detail about the debate whether Ps 119 or Ps 19 was first and concludes again that Ps 119 was first.

46. Zinner lists them: "The sequence *torah,ʿ edut, piqqud, miṣwah*, and *mišpaṭ* in Ps 19:8-6 is manifestly borrowed from Ps 119's ʾAlef strophe, whose sequence is *torah* (v. 1), *ʿ edot* (v. 2), *piqqud* (v. 4), *ḥoq* (v. 5), *miṣwah* (v. 6),

the six subjects in the construct chain with *YHWH* in Ps 19:7–9, all but *yr?h* 'fear' in 19:9 are keywords with around 22 repeats in Ps 119.⁴⁷ "Fear" comes as a noun once in Ps 119:38 with "you" as the object, and as a verb in Ps 119 with the object "you" for God three times, and once for "your judgments" in 119:120. Why would the author of Ps 19 choose "fear of the Lord" in the list of Torah subjects and give special focus to it by accompanying it with lemmas with high alphabetical counts, when it is not used as a Torah keyword in Ps 119? Zinner proposes that the devotion given to the Torah at the time of Ezra could have been "watered down" by a later emphasis on "the fear of the Lord" in Ps 19, and as later found repeatedly in Sirach 1.⁴⁸

The high counts for 9A with "fear of the Lord" are significant. In the above Tables 2 and 5 with alphabetical counts, 9A has the highest ratios for both lemmas (100%) and factors (166.67%

---

mišpaṭ (v. 7). Ps 19 omits 119:5's *ḥoq*, substituting it with *yirah*". (Yoder and Zinner, *Psalm 119*, 76).

47. Freedman *(Psalm 119*, 32–35) lists the eight keywords in Ps 119 with their frequencies. The two not found in Ps 19 are *'imrâ* 'saying' 19 times in Ps 119, and *ḥōq* 'statute' 22 times. *Dbr* 'word', which occurs in Ps 19:3, is also one of the keywords with 22 repeats in Ps 119. It has the YHWH=26 alphabetical value. Of the two that do not occur in Ps 19, *?mrh* 'word' has the alphabetical value of 39 (13x3, and 26+13), and *ḥq* 'saying' has the alphabetical value of 25 (5x5). None of the three that do not occur in Ps 19:7-9 have mathematical symbolic values.

48. Zinner ("Psalm 19," 46) also writes, "Ps 119 does not know of "Fear of the Lord" as a Torah title or key Torah term as does Ps 19. Ps 19's trope of the fear of the LORD as a Torah attribute is therefore much more developed than what we encounter in Ps 119". Zinner ("Psalm 19," 46-47) credits Grund (*Psalm 19 im Kontext der nachexilischen Toraweisheit*) and Klein ("Half Way Between Psalm 119 and Ben Sira: Wisdom and Torah in Psalm 19") with showing the uniqueness of Ps 19's "Fear of the LORD" as a postexilic development contrasting with Ps 119. Klein ("Half Way Between", 9) writes, "The author of Ps 119 apparently knows fear as the adequate mind-set towards the divine law (cf. 119:120), but only his successor in Ps 19 goes so far as to transform the moral quality itself into a variation of torah." Although Zinner and Yoder on p. 24 note that Grund and Klein hold a "minority view on this issue," Zinner (*Psalm 119*, 91) concludes his thorough 2020 evaluation of both sides of the question of precedence by stating, "Grund's and Klein's arguments for Ps 19's dependence on Ps 119 seem more plausible, balanced, and secure."

and 175%). The position of *yr?h* 'fear' in Ps 19 is also numerically significant. It comes 52nd from the end of Ps 19, which is significant since 52=26x2. This is important to note since *twrh* 'law', the first word of the second poem, is 52 words from the beginning of the poetic lines. This adds significance to "fear of the Lord" to be matched with the initial "law of the Lord" by their juxtaposed numerical positions. As noted in the "Line by Line Analysis of Ps 19," 9A is unique with the theological *YHWH* factors 6-6, 26-13, and 10-5 duplicated in both alphabetical and mathematical counts in spite of different totals for "fear" and "pure"—*yr?h* 'fear'=**36** (**6x6**) [**216** 6x36, or 6x6x6], *yhwh*=**26** (x1, **13x2**) [**26**x1, **13x2**], *thwr* 'pure'=**40** (**10x4**, **5x20**) [**220** 10x22, 5x44, **11**x20]. The colon total for 9Aa is also powerful with alphabetical 102=17x6 having the short count for *YHWH*, 17, together with 6=W of *YHWH*, and mathematical 462=6x77, 7x66, 22x21, and 11x42 with many factors of the 22-set as well as 6 and 7. The alphabetical total for the whole v. 7 brings the 17-symbolism to a peak with 289=17x17. The values of the lemma *thwr* 'pure', which describes "fear of the Lord" are especially potent with alphabetic 40=10x4 and 5x20, and mathematical 220=10x22, 5x44, and 11x20, with both having factors of 10 and 5 for YH. This is also the only time where the adjective *thwr* 'clean/pure' is applied to "fear of the Lord" in the Hebrew Bible, suggesting a choice here of a high numerically symbolic lemma.[49]

The location of *ʕdwt* 'decrees' in both Pss 19 and 119 is significant. As noted above in the discussion "V. 7B", the central phrase in Ps 119:88—*ʕdwt pyk* 'decrees of your mouth'—is highly marked by coming as the central two words of Ps 119. Yoder and Zinner pointed to the special importance of *ʕdwt*, noting its "lynchpin role".[50] The placement of *ʕdwt* in the center complements the beginning-to-center repetition resulting from v. 2 as the first keyword after "Torah" in the first stanza of Ps 119. "Torah" and *ʕdwt* are further related by having the same first acrostic word, *ʔšry*

---

49. Zinner (*Psalm 119*, 76) gives another possible reason for the choice of טָהוֹר: "*ṭehorah*, a play on *torah*".

50. Yoder and Zinner (*Psalm 119*, 32).

'happy'. The Ps 119 placement of ʿdwt is followed in Ps 19, where it is the first keyword after Torah in v. 7B.

One reason why ʿdwt could have been chosen for this distinguished placement is its numerical value. It is the Torah keyword in Psalm 19 with the *highest symbolic count*. It has the beautiful mathematical value of 480 with factors of 32x15, 10x48, 6x80, and 5x96. These include the divine-name number 32 from *kbwd* 'glory', and the YHWH numbers 10, 6, and 5. 480 also has the alphabetical value of 48 (6x8). ʿdwt and mšpṭ come 23 times in Ps 119 as the highest counts among the Torah keywords after Torah's 25. The alphabetical count for *kbwd* is 23, giving these two keywords further prominence as a divine-name number. The strategic placements of the numerically highly symbolic ʿdwt help to make the word of God in Psalm 19 "sweeter than honey."

The next keyword in both Ps 119:4 and Ps 19:8A is *pqwdym* 'precepts'. Amazingly, it has half of the mathematical value of ʿdwt's 480 with 240, and although it does not have a 32, it has the same YHWH numbers in the factors 10x24, 6x40, 5x48. The last keyword *mšpṭ* in 119:7 and coming with the highest five symbolic factors in 19:9B has the same YHWH numbers 10, 6, and 5, but in the factors of the alphabetical value 60 (10x6, 5x12). It also has mathematical 429 with factors 13x33, and 11x39, where 39 is especially symbolic since 39=26+13. *Yrʔh* 'fear' in Ps 19:9A has interesting sixes, with alphabetical 36 (6x6) and mathematical 216 (6x6x6). Only *mṣwt* 'commandment' in Ps 119:6 and Ps 19:8B, with values of alphabetical 59 and mathematical 536, have no symbolic factors.[51]

The lemma ʿd 'forever' is applied differently in Ps 19:9A and Ps 119. "Continue forever" (ʿd tmyd) is only applied to keeping the *twrh* 'law' in Ps 119, not anything else. See Ps 119:44 wʔšmrh twrtk tmyd lʿwlm wʿd "I will keep your law continually, forever and ever." The only other examples of ʿd in Ps 119 are three

---

51. "Statutes" (ḥq), which does not come in Ps 19, but comes in Ps 119:5 along with the six Torah keywords in its first stanza, has no symbolic mathematical factors with the value of 106, but has symbolic *alphabetical* factors 5x5 with the value of 25.

occurrences of the compound ʕd-mʔd meaning 'utterly'. However, in Ps 19:9A, "Enduring forever" (ʕwmdt lʕd) applies directly to "the fear of the Lord."

Studies of the chiastic structure of the psalms from Ps 15 to Ps 24 have identified Ps 19 as the center, and that this adds a "theological" perspective to the varied themes in all ten psalms.[52] This structural arrangement for theological purposes may also include what is proposed here in pointing to similarities and differences between Pss 19 and 119 as a theological emphasis on "fear of the Lord" in Ps 19:9A, indicated by its high symbolic counts.

Job 28:28 in the chapter describing where wisdom can be found is likely related to this special emphasis on "fear of the Lord." In the final v. 28, God addresses humankind, "Truly, the fear of the Lord, that is wisdom; and to depart from evil is understanding." Also note Ps 111:10 "The fear of the Lord is the beginning of wisdom; a good understanding have all those who practice it."[53]

In this analysis, 9A has the most alphabetical symbolic lemmas and factors of all 22 lines. It is proposed in this study that Ps 19 emphasizes "the fear of the Lord" as a highly important teaching, and that this is marked by having 9A with a plethora of symbolic numbers. This is an exception to the overall results in the study, which have found higher-than-average symbolic counts in places with structural prominence, such as peaks and peripheral lines. This can alert analysts to give attention to exceptions to patterns, which may point to goals secondary to the main themes of a text.

The enhancement of Ps 19 with symbolic numbers has truly helped to make its message and structure "sweeter than honey."

---

52. Sumpter ("Psalms 15–24," 186) credits Auffret ("Les Psaumes 15 à 24") as the first to describe this chiasmus in 1982, and gives a diagram of correspondences based on the genre of each psalm. In pp. 187–91 Sumpter critiques other studies of this chiastic group of psalms. On p. 192 he writes that the "framing" psalms 15, 19, and 24 provide an "ultimate theological context" for the intervening psalms.

53. Zinner (Ps *119*, 79–80) notes that although Ps 19 has been seen as prior to Ps 111, "one could just as well argue the reverse". Zinner points out: "It arguably makes sense that Ps 19:10 incorporated the phrase לָעַד עוֹמֶדֶת from Pss 111, 112, and 148 as the result of noticing its marked peculiar repetition in these three psalms."

Bibliography

Auffret, Pierre. "Les Psaumes 15 à 24 comme ensemble structuré," *La sagesse a bâti sa maison. Études de structures littéraires dans l'Ancien Testament et spécialement dans les psaumes.* (Fribourg, 1982).

Bekins, Peter. "The Omission of the Definite Article in Biblical Poetry." (Expanded version of paper presented at the Society of Biblical Literature Meeting in San Antonio, 2016) 1-26. (Accessed in www.academia.edu).

Biblia Hebraica Stuttgartensia. Edited by K. Elliger and W. Rudolph. (Stuttgart: Württembergische Bibelanstalt, 1969).

Bliese, Loren F. "Structurally Marked Peak in Psalms 1–24." *Occasional Papers in Translation and Textlinguistics* 4.4 (1990) 266–321. Online at www.sil.org/resources/; search for "Loren Bliese", then select this article, click on OPTAT_04(4).pdf, and scroll to the article.

———. "Symmetry and Prominence in Hebrew Poetry." In *Discourse Perspectives on Hebrew Poetry in the Scriptures.* Edited by Ernst R. Wendland. UBS Monograph Series, no. 7. (New York: United Bible Societies, 1994) 67-94.

———. *Count God In: Theological Numbers in the Song of Songs.* (Eugene: Wipf and Stock, 2018).

———. *God's Good Covenant: Poetic Beauty in Hosea Enhanced by Counting.* (Eugene: Wipf and Stock, 2021).

Brown, William P. "'Here Comes the Sun!' The Metaphorical Theology of Psalms 15–24," *The Composition of the Book of Psalms.* Edited by E. Zenger. (Leusen: *Bibliotheca Ephemeridum Theologicarum Lovaniensium,* no. 238, 2010) 259–277.

Craigie, Peter C. *Psalms 1–50. Word Biblical Commentary,* vol 19. (Dallas: Word, 1983).

Freedman, David Noel. *Psalm 119: The Exaltation of Torah.* (Winona Lake: Eisenbrauns, 1999).

Goldberg, Oskar. *Die Fünf Büches Moses: Ein Zahlengebäude.* (Typed academic paper, Berlin, 1908).

Goldengay, John. *Psalms: Psalms 1–41.* Vol 1. *Baker Commentary on the Old Testament Wisdom and Psalms.* (Grand Rapids: Baker, 2006).

Grund, Alexandra. "*Die Himmel erzählen die Ehre Gottes*": *Psalm 19 im Kontext der nachexilischen Toraweisheit.* (*Wissenschaftliche Monographien zum Alten und Neuen Testament,* no. 103; Neukirchen-Vluyn: Neukirchener Verlag, 2004).

BIBLIOGRAPHY

"Key Terms of the Old Testament." *Paratext*. (SIL and United Bible Societies.) (Online Bible Translation Program).

Klein, Anja. "Half Way between Psalm 119 and Ben Sira: Wisdom and Torah in Psalm 19." In *Wisdom and Torah: The Reception of Torah in the Wisdom Literature of the Second Temple Period. Supplements to the Journal for the Study of Judaism*, vol. 163. Edited by U. Schipper and A. Teeter. (Brill Academic, 2013) 119-136. http://www.brill.com/wisdom-and-torah. (Accessed in University of Edinburgh Research Explorer.)

Knohl, Israel. "Sacred Architecture: The Numerical Dimensions of Biblical Poems." *Vetus Testamentum* 62 (2012) 189–197. (Accessed in www.academia.edu).

Krawczyk, Arje Josef. "The Name, the Heights and the Number 26: The Significance of Gematria Method, Further Findings on Gematria 26 Structures within the Torah." *Kwartainik Historii Żydów* no. 2 (278) (2021, ISSN 1899-3034) 349-371. (Accessed in www.academia.edu).

Labuschagne, Casper, J. "Significant Compositional Techniques in the Psalms: Evidence for the Use of Number as an Organizing Principle." *Vetus Testamentum* 59 (2009) 583–605. (Accessed in www.academia.edu).

———. *Numerical Secrets of the Bible: Introduction to Biblical Arithmology*. (Eugene: Wipf and Stock, 2016).

———. "On the Structural Use of Numbers as a Composition Technique." *Journal of Northwest Semitic Languages*, 12 (1984[1986]) 87–99.

Lenzi, Alan, "The Metonic Cycle, Number Symbolism, and the Placement of Psalms 19 and 119 in the MT Psalter," *Journal for the Study of the Old Testament* 34.4 (2010) 447–473.

Mathis, Eric. "Commentary on Psalm 19." *Working Preacher*. (Posted January 24, 2016). https://www.workingpreacher.org.

Quinn, Carissa M. "A Methodology for the Cohesion of Psalms: Psalms 15, 19, and 24 as a Test Case." (Draft for a chapter of an edited volume titled, *Between the Psalms and the Twelve: Exploring the Nature and Shape of Composition*, Edited by Matt Ayars & Peter Ho.) (Accessed in www.academia.edu).

Sumpter, Philip. "The Coherence of Psalms 15–24." (Rome: Gregorian Biblical, 2013) 186–209. (Accessed in www.academia.edu).

Yoder, Keith L., and Zinner, Samuel. *Psalm 119's Eight Key Torah Terms' Intentional Gender-Based Distribution Patterns: Documenting "Cryptic" Gender-Matched Parallelism* (Draft Book, 2020) (University of Massachusetts, Amherst, Internet Data temporarily offline) (Accessed an email copy June 2025 from Samuel Zinner, the author of "2. Psalm 119's Theology" and "3. Dating Psalm 119", 43–91).

Ziemer, Benjamin. "Zahlen, Zahlensymbolik" *Wörterbuch alttestamentlicher Motive*. Edited by. M. Fieger, J. Krispenz and J. Lanckau. (Darmstadt: Wissenschaftliche Buchgesellschaft, 2013) 462–471. (Accessed in www.academia.edu).

Zinner, Samuel. "Chapter 6, Psalm 19's Literary and Chronological Unity: And the Straightforward and Acrostic Connections Between the Torah-Royal Pss 1-2, 18-19, 110-111, and 118-119." *Recovering Ancient Hebrew Scribal Numerical and Acrostic Techniques* (Draft Book, 2019) 1-48. (Accessed in www.academia.edu).

———. "Introduction." *Recovering Ancient Hebrew Scribal Numerical and Acrostic Techniques* (Draft Book, 2019) 1-31. (Accessed in www.academia.edu).

Author Index

Auffret, Pierre, 81n52, 83

Bekins, Peter, 40, 40n24–25, 41, 41n26, 83

Bliese, Loren, xxi-n5, 5n6, 6n9, 8n13, 11n19, 14n20, 70n38, 83

Brown, William, 20n22, 53n29, 83

Craigie, Peter, 6n8, 53n28, 75, 75n40, 76, 76n42, 77n43, 83

Freedman, David, xxi–4, 60n34, 78n47, 83

Goldberg, Oskar, 1n1, 83
Goldengay, John, 7n11, 7n12, 9n16, 59n32, 83
Grund, Alexandra, 78n48, 83

Klein, Anja, 6n7, 7n12, 78n48, 84
Knohl, Israel, xx–2, 84
Krawczyk, Arje, 1n1, 84

Labuschagne, Casper, xv, xxi–5, 3n5, 5n6, 84
Lenzi, Alan, xx–2, 77n44, 84

Mathis, Eric, 6n7, 84

Quinn, Carissa, 20n22, 21n23, 84

Schedl, Claus, 5n6
Sumpter, Philip, 81n52, 84

Yoder, Keith, 8, 8n14, 61n35, 78n46, 78n48, 79, 79n50, 84

Ziemer, Benjamin, 1n1, 6n10, 84
Zinner, Samuel, 1n2, 2n3, 6n7, 8, 8n14, 9n15, 9n17, 19n21, 54, 54n30, 59n33, 61n35, 61n37, 75n39, 75n41, 77, 77n44, 77n45, 77n46, 78, 78n48, 79, 79n49, 79n50, 81n53, 84, 85

Subject Index

Abridged, Key entries are **bold**

7, xv, xix-n**1**, 2–3, 14, 26–27, 33, 39–40, 53–54, 58, 60–61, 65–66

17, xx, **2**, **8**, 8n**13**, 13, 15, 17, 19, 31–32, 34, 39–40, 53–56, 61–62, 64, 67, 70, 73–74, 79

22, xv, xxi, xxi-n**4**, 2–4, 14, 19, 23–24, 26, 30, 32, 34, 36–40, 54, 57–58, 62–64, 67–69, 72–75, 77–78, 78n47, 79

23, **2**, **13**, 17, **19**, 33, 35, 39–41, 50, 55, 58, 60, 64–65, 68–72, 74, 76, 80

26, **x**, xv, xix, xix-n1, xx–xxi, 1n1, **2**, 3–4, **8**, 8n**13**, 11, **13**, 16–17, 22, **23–24**, 26–31, **32–33**, 35, **38**, 39–40, 42, 44–46, 49n27, 50, 52–55, 57–**58**, **59**, 63–**64**, **65–66**, 69–71, 74, **79**, 84

32, **2**, **13**, 15, **19**, 28–29, 34, **38**–40, 53, **56**, 60–**61**, 62–64, **68**, 70–73, **80**

39, xix-n1, 2, 3n**4**, **4–5**, 5n**6**, **15**, **17**–18, 23–24, 30–**32**, **33**, 53, **55**, 63–64, **66–67**, 78n47, 80

546, **xix**, xix-n1, **32–33**, 66

999, 38, **74**, 76

alphabet(ical), **ix** (chart), **1**, 3, 12–14, 17, 19, 23–26, 29, 39–40, 42, **43–44**, **50–51**, 63–65, **75**, 78, 81

analogy, **19**, 19n**21**, **20**, 20n**22**, 21n23, 50, 57–58

article(s), 40–41 (reduced in poetry), 65

buildup, **6**, 42, 64, **73–74**

chiasm(us), **7–9**, 20, 27, **65**, 81n52

climax, xx

cline, 5, **43–45**, **47–48**, **50–51**, 74

colon/cola, xxi-n**4** (explained), 5, 8–10, 30, 35, 40–42, 47, 50–52, 60–62, 66–69, 74

discontinuous bicolon, **7**, 18, 58

embellishment, **xix–xx**, xxi, 5, 10, 22, **52**, 55, 64–65, **75**

factors, xvi, **xix**, xix–**1**, 3–6, 9–10, 12–**14**, 17, 19, 24, 26, 40–41, **42**–43, 46, **50**, 56, 58–60, 63–66, 68, 74, 78–80

fear, xvi, 7–8, 7n12, 22, 30, 42–44, 49, **63**–64, 68, **76–81**, 78n**48**

gematria, xxi–5, **1**, 1n2, 19n21, 75n41, 84

gender pattern, **8**, 8n**14**, 84

globally unique referents, 40–**41**

high points, **xv**, **xix**, 6n7, **48–50**, 65

homogeneous, **6**, 6n**9**, **11**, **24**

SUBJECT INDEX

identical factors, **42** (in one lemma), 63 (in both 9Aa counts)

Kabbalah, 1, 1n1
kbwd, **2**, **13**, **19**, 55, 61, 64, 68, 70, **80**
keyword(s), **xx**, **2**, 8n13, 49n27, 60, 76–77, 78–**80**, 78n47, 80n51

lemma(s), **x**, **xv–xvi**, **xx–xxi**, 1n1, **2–4**, 5, **10–12**, 13–14, 14n20, 17, 19, **24–26**, 27, 32–33, 35, 38, 42–**44**, 46–**49**, 50–55, 58–60, 61n35, 62–**66**, 67–68, **74**–79, 81
lunar, 7n10, 77n44

Masoretic/MT, xiii, xx, 3, 11–**13**, 21, 42, 61n35, **66**, 77n44, 84
mathematical, **ix** (chart), x, xix, 1, 1n1, 2, **3–4**, 6, 8n13, 9, 12–15, 19, 21–22, 24–**26**, 28, 32–34, 38, 41–43, 45–50, 52–53, 56, 59–60, 61n35, 62–63, 65–**66**, 67–68, **74**–75, 76, 79–80
metaphor, **74–75**, 83
methodology, **1–5**, 108
metrical chiasm, 7, **8–9**, **65–66**

overall structure, **xvi**, **6–9**

parallelism: xx, **7–8**, 8n14, 15, 25, 33, 59, **65–66**, 84; (inverted 57), (numerical 24, 32, 54, 56, 61, 65, 67–**68**, 69)
Paratext, 61n36, 84
peak, xv, xix, 6n7, 83: (v. 10A chiastic, **xvi**, 7–**8**, **32–33**, 40–41, 49, **64–66**, 67, 69), (v. 6B final, **xvi**, xx, 6–7, 9–10, 18, 21, **24**, **26**, 48, 50, 53, **58**, 69), (vv. 4B and 14B secondary, **9**, 42–43, 49–52, **55**, 66, 72, 73–74)

person, 57 (third), 74 (first)
prominence, xx, 6n9, 8–11, **14**, 26–27, 33, 44, 46, 52, **54**, 57–58, **61–63**, **66–67**, 68, 72, **74–75**, 80–81, 83

repetition, **xxi**, 5, **8–9**, 24, **32**, **53**, 58–**59**, 79, 81n53

short line, **6–7**, **9**, **19**, 42, **55**
stanza, **xvi**, 7, 12, 18–19, 21–22, **34**, 41–42, 48, **55–56**, 58, 67–68, 77, 80n51
strophe, **xvi**, 7, 16, **18**, **29**, **32**, **34**, 72, 77, 77n46
sweet(er, -ness), **xix–xx**, xix–1, **32–33**, 63, **66**, 80–81

terrace series, 6
textual variant *mʕśy* 'work', 42
theological (numbers), xv, **2–3**, 5n6, 13–14, 17, **22–23**, 25–**26**, **28**, **39–40**, 52, **54–55**, **59**, 63, 70–71, 73, 79, **81**, 81n52
Torah, xvi, **xix–xx**, 3n5, 6n8, **7–8**, 10, **42**, **46–47**, 53n28, 60–61, 60n34, 63, **66**, 77, 77n46, **78**, 78n48, 79–**80**, 83–85

value(s), **ix–x**, **xv**, **xix**, xxi, **1–4**, 8, 8n13, **11–13**, 15, 20, **24–26**, **32–33**, **42–43**, **50**, **53–54**, 56–58, 59–61, 61n35, 62–63, **64–66**, **74–75**, 78n47, **79–80**

Wisdom, **xix**, 7n12, 10, 24, **54**, **61**, **69–71**, 76–77, 76n42, 78n48, **81**, 83–84
word-stress, stress, **12**, 66

Scripture Index

Abridged, Key entries are **bold**

Genesis

10:21–29
19:23   57

Exodus

3:14   2

Deuteronomy

6:4   5

Joshua

19:14   57

2 Kings

11:12   61

1 Chronicles

17:5   56

Job

28:28   7–8, 81

Psalms

15–24   20, 20n22, 53
15:1   20, 20n22, 56
15:2   53
18   60
18:2   9, 75n39
19:1–14   77
19:1–6   xvi, **6**, 12, 25–26, 39–40, 58
19:1   4, 6, **14**, 16–18, 19n21, 23, 25, 40, 42, 44–45, **52–53**
19:2   3, 6, 7n10, 9, **15–16**, 24, 45, **53–54**, 79
19:3–4   xx, 26, 42
19:3   78n47, 9, **16–17**, 42, **54**–55
19:4–6   6, 21n23, 25
19:4   3, 7, 7n10, **18–20**, 19n21, 21, 24, 42, **55–56**, 57
19:5   20–21, **22–23**, 7n10, 50, 55, **56–57**
19:6–8   **9–11**, 27
19:6   xvi, xxi, 6n8, 7n10, 10, 21, **24–25**, 26, 42, 49, 53, **57–58**, 60, 69
19:7–14   xvi, **7–8**, 27, 39–40, 46, 66

SCRIPTURE INDEX

Psalms *(continued)*

19:7–11	7n12
19:7–9	7n12, 8, 8n14, 59, 77–78, 77n46, 78n47
19:7–8	10, 68
19:7	8, 10, **28–29**, 42, 44, 46, 49n27, **59–61**, 61n37, 64, 68, 70, 80, 79–80
19:8	4, 9, **29–30**, 31, **62–63**, 64, 68, 80
19:9	xvi, 6n7, 8, 22, **30–31**, 42–43, 49, 51, 54, 60, **63–64**, 66–67, 77–78, 80–81
19:10	xix, 6n7, 7–8, **32–33**, 48–49, 63, **64–67**, 81
19:11–14	59
19:11–13	73
19:11	8, 17, 34, 48–49, **67–68**, 69–70, 76
19:12–14	53
19:12–13	21n23
19:12	xvi, 9–10, 10n18, 21, 24–25, **35–36**, 60, **68–71**, 72–74
19:13–14	74
19:13	**36–37, 71–73**, 74
19:14	**37–38**, 43, 49, 52–53, **73–75**, 76
24:8	20

78:35	75
93:5	60
107:43	69–70, 71
111:10	81
119	60, 60n34, 64, 78
119:1–7	77, 77–78n46
119:1	60
119:4	80
119:5	77, 78n46, 80n51
119:6	80
119:7	80
119:38	78
119:44	80
119:72	66
119:80	53
119:88	60, 61n35, 79
119:103	32
119:120	78, 78n48
119:127	66
119:130	61
119:154	75n39
143: 2	64

Proverbs

1:7	7n12, 54
2:5	7n12
9:10	7n12
15:13	7n12
21:11	61

Isaiah

62:5	20

Jeremiah

1:16	42
16:17	21

Hosea

3:5	2–3n4
5:6	71
7:16	2–3n4
8:1–3	8n13
14:7	2–3n4
14:9	69–70, 70n38, 71

Amos

9:3	21

www.ingramcontent.com/pod-product-compliance
Lightning Source LLC
Chambersburg PA
CBHW072158100426
42738CB00011BA/2462